SALT-GLAZED CERAMICS

The Stone Crock

In my hand I hold
a postcard
addressed to me
   by a lady

Stoneware crock
salt-glazed
a dandelion embossed
   dark blue

She selected it
for me to
admire casually
   in passing

she was a Jewess
intimate of
a man I
   admired

We often met in
her studio
and talked
   of him

he loved the early
art of this
country
   blue stoneware

stamped on the
bulge of it
Albany reminding me
   of him

Now he is dead how
gentle he
was and
   persistent

SALT-GLAZED CERAMICS

BY JACK TROY

WATSON-GUPTILL PUBLICATIONS / NEW YORK

PITMAN PUBLISHING / LONDON

*(Frontis) Stoneware crock, Albany, New York. 19th century.
National Gallery of Art, Washington, Index of American De-
sign. Watercolor rendering by John Tarantino. Poem from*
William Carlos Williams, Pictures from Brueghel. *Copyright ©
1962 by William Carlos Williams. Reprinted by permission of
New Directions Publishing Corporation.*

First published 1977 in the United States and Canada by Watson-Guptill Publications,
a division of Billboard Publications, Inc.
1515 Broadway, New York, New York 10036

Library of Congress Cataloging in Publication Data
Troy, Jack, 1938–
    Salt-glazed ceramics.
    Bibliography: p.
    Includes index.
    1. Glazing (Ceramics) I. Title.
TT922.T76   738.1'44   76-53036
ISBN O-8230-4630-3

Published in Great Britain by Pitman Publishing Ltd.
39 Parker Street, London WC2B 5PB
ISBN O-273-01053-0

Manufactured in U.S.A.

First printing, 1977

Edited by Sarah Bodine
Designed by Bob Fillie
Set in 10 pt. Helvetica Light by Publishers Graphics, Inc.
Printed and bound by Interstate Book Manufacturers, Inc.
Color printed by Toppan Printing Corp. America

To the memory of Jim Kietzman,
my first teacher.
Gentle . . . persistent.

Jar made at the Giertz Pottery, Aden-dorf, Germany. 12'' (30 cm). About 1840–1900. Stoneware. Collection of Sammlung J. Hansen, Adendorf.

CONTENTS

*Vase form by Don Reitz, Wisconsin. 18''
(45.7 cm). Stoneware, sprayed oxide
and iron glaze decoration.*

FOREWORD

Dear Jack,

Can't for the life of me figure out how you managed to sit on your posterior and assemble this compendium of facts on salt glazing. I remember those long hours we sat down by the kiln on the farm discussing (arguing) about the validity of such a book. As I recall, my major concern and argument was that if someone really wanted to find out about salt, they would, in spite of the lack of published material. I had fears that such a book might get in the way of gut experimentation and the practical kinds of risk-taking that books can inhibit. However, I wonder just how much unnecessary experimenting I did, and how many "dumb" things I would not have had to do, if I would have been aware of more written information than Dan's paragraph.

I am concerned about the tendency to use salt glazing as an easy answer. The old axiom, ''If it doesn't work, refire; if it still doesn't work—salt,'' misinterprets the virtues of the salting process. My biggest disappointment is watching people waste their time with salt, when in fact their work has nothing to do with it. The reason for using salt is that the work demands it; it is dependent upon it; it suffers without it. One does not make a pot for salt, but rather salt if required by the object. One does not simply throw salt into the fire to see how much sodium can be heaped onto the ware. It is more than an exercise in technique and surface activity. Each piece requires different amounts of sodium. It is knowing how to use the kiln as a tool that is important. It is the realization that salt glazing can be a complete synthesis of ma-

terial, process, and idea. It is a way of thinking. It is the visual interpretation of one's own awareness.

As you know, salt glazing is not a singular activity or technique. As the idea comes to fruition, so will all the processes and techniques required for its completion become clear. Each step is dependent upon the previous one. Choosing the clay, forming methods, surface treatments, stacking the kiln so that each piece is placed to best advantage, the type of atmosphere and temperature at which the kiln will be fired, what kind and how much salt to use, all are aspects of the process that anticipate the grand finale. However, in the process, new ideas and possibilities are unleashed that render yesterday's objects obsolete.

The historical section of your book brought many new pieces of information to me. I remember you saying that if knowledge is recorded it does not become lost in time. Because a great number of people are now experimenting with salt glazing, your book comes to us at a most opportune time. I am happy you stuck to your original idea and made the book a documenting device for the practical trial and error experimentation that is going on at the grass roots level throughout the country. I found this book neither dictatorial nor tedious. I find it a factual compendium on salt glazing, leaving the reader with concepts to deal with rather than rules. I applaud your ability, enthusiasm, and perseverance in such a worthwhile undertaking.

Madison, Wisconsin

PREFACE

On September 2, 1973, Don Reitz and I spent three days together loading and firing his salt kiln, going over the results, and planning the shape of this book. We organized basic chapters, and in my notes I wrote that we agreed '' . . . its thrust should be historical-factual-contemporary; balanced so as to appeal to a fairly diverse readership.''

Both of us were so involved with teaching and the production of our own work that writing became easier to put off as the winter and spring came and went and publishers looked over the outline. (Ceramics being done with the whole self, while writing involves mostly ones posterior, an arm, and the head, the sedentary hours at a desk held almost no appeal compared to the kinetic possibilities of days and nights in the studio.) I was designing and building a house, and when there weren't bowls to trim or kilns to stack, there was a class project to complete or a stairway to build. When I did make time to write, it was frustrating to find that unlike a decently thrown pot which needs no trimming, my prose was as clunky and overweight as my first enclosed forms and needed a lot of paring down. Eventually, though, I came to agree with whoever it was who said, ''I hate to write, but I love to have written.'' There was encouragement from friends and the challenge of stepping back from intuitive procedures and objectifying them; asking why certain pots appeared as they did, coming from the kiln; then trying to put the knowledge gained into readable form. Although only about 20%-30% of my ceramics production is in salt glaze, I have a renewed enthusiasm for the medium from having been close to it in a verbal as well as a tactile manner.

It began in 1969 when I got the mumps and couldn't go to the NCECA Conference in Kansas City. Bill Grosch, with whom I was to go, returned with descriptions of Don's work that stimulated my imagination, causing me to find out more about the method from David DonTigney at Penn State, and to build a salt kiln. Firing after firing was disgusting (I might as well have put brown shoe polish on my pots), and there seemed no good reasons to go on except for two: the knowledge that others were getting good results and an exhilarating sense of working in cahoots with fire. My first pots had been heated in electric kilns, and later were fired with gas, but the salt-firing process, with its activities,Z judgments, and hunches, introduced other elements into the ceramics experience which helped develop a stronger sense of identity with the fired objects. My pots improved as the kiln—the largest and most complex tool I had ever used—became seasoned, and my understanding of the process seemed to develop at a rate that I could comprehend and translate into new efforts.

In addition to gaining technical insights, I met Dean Reynolds, of Huntingdon, Pa., whose love for the early pottery of the country in which we live led me to an appreciation of my heritage. This feeling deepened when Gordon and Nancy Shedd located the base of a salt kiln built in the 1870s, only a few miles from our homes; and we visited it like pilgrims—bushels of shards under a few inches of topsoil, celadon-hued floor brick glazed into place, the flues now the home of a woodchuck—helping me see beyond the revolving disc of my own potter's wheel.

Barbara Sterne—a friend and former student—had worked at the Crozelius Pottery in Adendorf, Germany, and encouraged me to visit the country where salt glazing originated.

Taking a leave from my part-time job during 1975–1976 enabled me to travel and write between workshops and other short-term teaching assignments; and gradually, the book took form—in Council Grove, Montana; Eugene, Oregon; Berkeley, California; Baton Rouge, Louisiana; Lewisburg, Pennsylvania; Penland, North Carolina; Peters Valley, New Jersey; and in the south-facing loft of the new house.

I was determined to write a strictly nonfiction ceramics book containing historical and technical data as well as high-quality photos. (It seemed entirely possible to do this without a single photograph of disembodied hands squirting a syringe, attaching a spout, pointing in a kiln, or pinching a coil.) There was clearly no need for a ''philosophy of salt glazing'' apart from writing a book about it or throwing salt in my own kiln, and I can thank Daniel Rhodes for his terse advice over Andrée Thompson's phone one December evening in Berkeley: ''A whole *book* about salt glazing? It's only another kind of glaze . . . it's not a way of life.''

In May, 1976, a visit to Germany provided a glimpse of the extent to which salt glazing continues to be produced, and there were also instructive visits to museums. Helga Ward, who drove and translated, was patient and amazingly efficient, and I attribute most of the success of my trip directly to her.

The following German potters were generous in shar-

Wooden ark with its crew. These stoneware sales vessels floated down the Monongahela, Ohio, and Mississippi around 1870, docking at towns along the way to sell wares. Photo: Collection, Center for Prehistoric and Historic Archeology, California State College, California, Pa.

ing their homes, studios, and knowledge of salt glazing: Karl Corzelius, Hubert Neukirchen, Eugen Braun, Joachim Hansen, Wilhelm Mühlendyck, and Richard Zinko.

The staffs of the followint museums were particularly helpful: Staatliche Ingenieurschule and Werkschule für Keramik, Höhr-Grenzhausen; Rheinisches Landesmuseum, Bonn; Dr. Von Boch at the Kunstgewerbe museum, Eigelsteintorborg, Cologne; Dr. Klinge at the Hetjens Museum, Düsseldorf; and particularly to the staff of the magnificent ceramics gallery in Frechen, Keramion, for their time and gifts nf books.

Dr. Cornelius Frijters of Juniata College provided considerable assistance in translating from time to time, and Alex McBride, another colleague, helped greatly with photography.

Nancy Sweezy, Vernon Owens, Dorothy and Walter Auman, and Dr. Georgeanna Greer were most helpful in providing current and background information on Southern stoneware.

Spencer Davis acquainted me with the simple fact that a book reaches far more persons than 100 workshops, classes, or pots, and I thank him for that.

Daniel Rhodes, Don Reitz, and Norm Schulman read portions of the manuscript and made helpful comments.

Warren MacKenzie provided information on the potteries in La Borne, France, which I visited.

I am indebted to Richard Leach of Albion, Michigan for his contribution of photos and written information regarding castable kilns.

Many of my students have contributed to this book by way of their enthusiasm, and I want to thank them, particularly—too many to name individually.

Marsha Davis was an efficient, reliable typist.

Sarah Bodine, Associate Ceramics Editor at Watson-Guptill, has been patient and most helpful throughout the project. It has been a pleasure as a potter and writer to work professionally with a potter and editor.

The 5,000 copies of the first edition of this book took approximately 2 tons of paper, and I wish to acknowledge the 35 or so trees which were cut down to make it possible.

Sharing and participating in the project on many levels, from that of disinterested critic and able librarian to rare companion over varied terrain, has been Loanne Snavely. Uppercase Thanks to her.

CHAPTER ONE
ORIGINS OF SALT-GLAZING TECHNIQUE

Salt glazing is known to have originated in Germany's Rhineland, and various sources attribute its discovery from as early as the 12th to as late as the 15th century. Although we may never know precisely which person or group was responsible for the discovery, or how it came about, several factors were necessary to set the stage: (1) rich natural resources, most importantly vast beds of excellent, easily prepared clays; (2) an abundance of wood for fuel; and (3) knowledge of high-firing kilns.

Advent of Stoneware

Pottery had been made on a large scale in the Rhine Valley since around the 7th century, so the awareness of suitable clays was known well in advance of the high-firing methods developed between 1000 and 1200 A.D., when stoneware, or *Steinzeug*, was first made in Europe.

The strength and durability of stoneware has always made it a highly practical commodity. One can only imagine the surprise and wonder which must have attended opening the first high-firing kilns—dating to about 500 B.C. in China. The sharp ringing of the pieces when they were struck was truly a new sound in history, and the advantages of such ware must have been obvious from the beginning. Since true stoneware is impervious to liquids, there was no necessity to develop high-fire glazes, as in the case of porous earthenware, but washes of fusible red clays were sometimes used to smooth the surfaces of pieces, which were at times pitted.

Discovery of Salt as a Glaze Material

Much speculation has arisen as to why potters began the rather unnatural practice of throwing salt into their kilns to produce glaze on the wares. There are many theories, but until a systematic study is undertaken, no conclusions can be considered airtight.

One theory advanced by a European scholar suggests that salt was used to keep red clay slips in suspension and that the sodium was sufficient to produce a faint glaze during the firing. No experiments have shown this to be the case, to my knowledge, however, and there is no solution advanced as to why salt was thrown into or placed within the kiln itself. Also, red clays in particular do not take vapor glaze especially well and, it seems, would require more sodium than would be present in such a slip. Nevertheless, it is a possibility.

Old Siegburg ware. 3'' to 8'' (7.6 to 20.3 cm) high. Vitreous stoneware, vapor glazed in irregularly flashed patterns. As early as the 15th century German wares exhibited sureness of form. Rheinisches Landesmuseum, Bonn.

Drinking vessel. 9'' (22.9 cm). Cologne-Frechen-Raeren area. About 1500. Kunstgewerbemuseum, Cologne.

Another suggestion is that wood from old salt-impregnated fish-storage or sauerkraut barrels was used to fire the kilns. It seems feasible that if such fuel were employed during the late stages of firing, potters might well have concluded from the results that salt had played a part in whatever differences were apparent in the fired objects. It is possible to introduce sodium into the atmosphere of a firing kiln in this manner (see Chapter 7 under Methods of Introduction), and, assuming the receptivity of the clay, glaze might well have formed under such conditions.

Perhaps, also, we should not dismiss the unlikely possibility that someone, in a moment of madness, pranksterism, or spite, threw salt, a commodity in wide use, into a kiln at a high temperature, with unprecedented results. (This could have happened within an hour or two after the firing had been concluded—when a kiln might be unattended—and vapor glazing could still have taken place.) Such a dramatic act, however, is likely to have been recorded, and to my knowledge it is not.

There seems, in addition, to be a transitional phenomenon in which certain clays, when exposed to specific kinds of wood ash at stoneware temperatures, will exhibit glaze effects which challenge one's capacity to distinguish them from salt glaze. In the Kunstgewerbemuseum, Eigelsteintorburg, Cologne, are several early pieces from the Siegburg potteries which seem salt-glazed in that the quality of the smooth surface appears to have formed from sodium vapors. The localized pattern in which it appears, however, and the lack of shaded, less glazed surfaces suggest that wood ash, perhaps containing sodium, was responsible. All this may simply show that glass-formers whose effect is similar to that of sodium itself (which normally occurs in ashes only in minute amounts), may be present in wood ash in sufficient quantity to produce a glaze like that made from vaporous salt. German potters made little use of that knowledge, however, since there is nothing to suggest their systematic use of ash in glazes, as was done in China. Interestingly enough, the circumstances attending the discovery of sodium vapor glazing apparently did not occur in the Orient. It may be that Shoji Hamada's salt kiln built in 1952 in Mashiko, Japan, was the first in the East.

If conclusive evidence is established about the origins of salt glazing, it will no doubt be produced by contemporary ceramists working closely with art historians and

The Peasant Dance *by Peter Brueghel (1530–1569). Detail. Kunsthistorisches Museum, Vienna, Austria.*

laboratory technicians. There is ample opportunity for research along these lines; and I wish, for my own satisfaction, to someday know more than I presently do about these matters.

Development in Germany

Some of the cities whose pottery traditions date to the Middle Ages, and which figured strongly in the development of stoneware production, are Siegburg, Cologne (or Köln), Frechen (nearby), Raeren, and Grenzhausen. Prior to stoneware, a hard, semivitreous ware was produced, reflecting Roman forms.

According to Sparkes and Gandy, "The earliest dated piece glazed with salt is a fragment of Raeren ware dated 1539. . . . The necessary salt was, no doubt, acquired through the Low Countries, and it is said that the red salt, in which New Foundland fish had been preserved was thought the best."[1] Quite likely, salt-glazed ware was being produced as early as the 1300s, but, in any case, by the mid-1500s, potters in Siegburg had formed a strong trade union, and it is apparent that the development of salt-glazed stoneware and the brewing industry were closely related.

Around 1500, as the use of hops in malt liquors gained popularity, inns and taverns developed, creating a demand for drinking vessels. A favorite shape made by Siegburg potters was the *Schnelle*—a long tankard for beer, whose name means "fast-goer" and evidently refers to the proper way to drink the contents. (Some historians have noted that the Reformation and hops in beer came in together.)

The pottery industry was quick to respond to the public's preference for stoneware over earthenware or metal tankards, and, in the case of the potters at Siegburg, careful regulation of their activities was practiced. The rules allowed them to work only certain months of the year and to make only a specified number of pieces at a given time. They permitted strangers to work at only the coarsest tasks, and their hard-earned knowledge was guarded jealously. Since the potters were Catholics, tithes were levied by the Catholic abbots on all the pots made.

As the Reformation spread through Germany, the Siegburg potters, though remaining Catholics, had no objection to making pots for the Protestants but would occasionally be fined by their ecclesiastical rulers for an especially flagrant offense. This trade came to an end early in the 17th century, when the Thirty Years War (1618–1648) between Catholics and Protestants disrupted all of Germany.

Siegburg ware is characterized by the presence of throwing marks, a pinched "pie-crust" type of foot, and vigorous, tall shapes. Similar pots appear in the paintings of Pieter Brueghel (1520?–1569), such as "The Wedding Banquet" (1568) and "The Peasant Dance" (1568). Both paintings depict wares which have been flashed in firing and show signs of small stones or bits of organic matter which caused surface blemishes, common in the country pottery of that day, known now as "early Siegburg," which was produced prior to 1400. In the mid-1500s white-burning stoneware clays were developed, and elaborate molded relief friezes, often copies from engravings, became common motifs, especially on tankards.

Raeren ware, from Raeren in the Low Countries, is a brown type of salt-glazed pottery, sometimes taking on the quality and color of bronze, probably owing to the presence of iron-bearing clay. Sectional throwing was perfected at Raeren, and many of the jugs produced there were made from three separate sections joined and rethrown to complete a form.

Cologne (Köln) ware was similarly dark, although some light-burning clays were also produced. A favorite decorative motif emulated precious stones in metal settings. Cologne ware was artistically important by 1520, but owing to feuds between town authorities and potters during the second half of the 16th century the industry moved to nearby Frechen. Some authors attribute the ill feelings to kiln vapors, others to "conflagrations" caused by the kilns. By 1650 the industry at Frechen rivaled that at Raeren, and to this day some of Germany's largest ceramics manufacturers are located there.

Kannenbächerland, or "Country of Potmakers," is a fourth German salt-glazing region. Grenzhausen, in the Westerwald area, just northeast of Koblenz, is where many potters fled to escape the horrors of the religiously inspired Thirty Years War. Pottery traditions in this locale, however, were strong, and Siegburg-type ware was made by the emigrant Anno Knutgen and his sons in Höhr (Westerwald) between 1570 and 1590.

The influx of new potters caused a quickening of the pulse of Westerwald ceramic traditions. Clays found

(Left) Spouted pitcher with hinged lid. 13" (34.5 cm). Cologne. Dated 1539. Complex textural patterns formed in press molds were favorites of potters, who borrowed the method from engravers. The clay is bronzelike in color. Rheinisches Landesmuseum, Bonn.

(Right) Siegburg Schnelle with pewter lid. 10" (25 cm). Dated 1590. White-burning clays were discovered in the Siegburg area after vapor glazing had been done first on darker stoneware clays. Rheinisches Landesmuseum, Bonn.

(Below) Detail from Siegburg Schnelle. About 1600. Rheinisches Landesmuseum, Bonn.

Three views of a Siegburg Schnelle with gold fittings. 1560. Biblical and historical scenes were often depicted on these drinking vessels. The word "Schnelle" means "fast-goer" and refers to the manner in which the contents are to be emptied. Rheinisches Landesmuseum, Bonn.

there burned to a gray or blue-gray color, as well as brown like those of Cologne. However, the lighter gray clays seem to have become favored, perhaps because they provided greater contrast to the cobalt-blue and manganese-purple decorations brought in by the new settlers. With the development of the Westerwald salt-glaze tradition came a transition away from the friezes and engraving-inspired relief designs of Raeren ware toward more colorful surfaces characterized by brush decoration and bird and floral motifs.

Kneussen (Bavaria) ware was the most elaborate and costly salt-glaze pottery of this period, as the influx of Italian majolica ware had inspired ceramists to develop low-fire opaque lead glazes known as enamels. This technique was applied as overglaze to previously fired salt-glazed wares, and between 1620 and 1750 it became a popular and influential medium in France and England as well.

Contemporary German Salt-glazed Work
German salt-glazed stoneware, saltzglaiser steinzeug, continues to be produced in huge quantities, both industrially and by studio potters.

Westerwald ceramic traditions flourish today, and the visitor to the village of Höhr-Grenzhausen, where there were 22 potteries in 1976, will be quick to notice signs of ceramic activity everywhere. Glass showcases displaying contemporary work can be seen on the main streets; a large ceramics education facility exists there (the Staatliche Ingenieurschule und Werkschule für Keramik), and the ''Potters' Hotel'' and ''Potters' Drugstore'' are evident. Many studio potters reside here and in neighboring villages, and ceramics industries of all kinds seem to flourish side by side. Some of Europe's finest clay-processing equipment is designed and produced in Höhr-Grenzhausen.

The formal training period for potters in Germany may last as long as 7 years, during which students receive intensive training in business management, machinery maintenance, clay processing, production methods, and technical studies. Rigorous exams are administered, and diplomas are proudly displayed by those who earn them, for they represent a great deal of difficult work and remain a kind of passport for teaching credibility and the sale of one's work.

German salt-glaze production is of the most con-

(Left) Jug by Engel Kran. 17¼'' (43.8 cm). Raeren ware. 16th century (1584). Stoneware. The Metropolitan Museum of Art, Gift of R. Thornton Wilson, 1954, in memory of Florence Ellsworth Wilson.

Bellarmine (or Bartmann) jug, salt-glazed stoneware. Cologne (Frechen), Germany, late 16th century. Light brown with spots of cobalt blue. The Metropolitan Museum of Art, Rogers Fund, 1910.

*(Right) Church-tower finial. 39½'' (100 cm).
Late 17th to early 18th century. Westerwald. Kunstgewerbemuseum, Cologne.*

*(Below) Plate. 13'' (33 cm). Westerwald.
1700s. Early wares made in the Höhr-
Grenzhausen area are characterized by vigorous decorative motifs executed in cobalt and
sgraffito. Kunstgewerbemuseum, Cologne.*

*(Bottom) Globular drinking vessel. 8'' (21
cm). 17th century. Cobalt slip decoration and
sprigged textures. Kunstgewerbemuseum,
Cologne.*

*Writing stand with penholder, inkwells,
and sand shaker. 10″ (25.4 cm). 18th
century. German. Keramion Gallery for
Ceramic Art, Frechen.*

"Originally I only strove for form. I started potting without ever having done any drawing or painting; then I came to the Westerwald and in my landlady's house I saw a few old pots. She still had some old tools, and I tried to work out for myself the old techniques of decorating pots . . . the "Kneibis" (sgraffito; incising). Doing that, I discovered that one cannot express with the form alone all that needs to be said with the heart.

"At first there was my love of flowers and animals. I tried to express in simple lines that which to me seems essential in an animal or flower. . . . Later, when religious feelings awakened in me, I had to entrust these also to the jugs and plates and bottles.

"I always say to the young people of today: 'Do you know why I draw those flowers and animals on my pots? Because I find God's creation beautiful.'"

Interview, May 21, 1976, Höhr-Grenzhausen. Helga P. Ward, translator.

Vase by Wilhelm Mühlendyck. 16" (40 cm). 1975. Incised and slip decorated.

Wall tile by Wilhelm Mühlendyck, Höhr-Grenzhausen. The availability of commercially made tiles in some German towns is of considerable advantage to potters, who buy them as greenware, decorate, and fire them.

sistently high quality anywhere in the world. The virtual perfection of methodology and the practice of high work standards in every aspect of shop management are evident to a visitor. Most prosperous potteries in Germany are run with an almost startling air of diligence and efficiency. Ram presses (high-speed pressure molding devices) have been in wide use since the 1950s, and the production of 1,000 pieces a day in a pottery employing four persons is not at all uncommon.

Clay at the Karl Corzelius Pottery in Adendorf, near Bonn, where there were 14 potters in 1976, is dug locally and slaked down in the corner of a room, in a pile perhaps 6½ ft high by 10 ft deep and wide (2m high by 3m deep and wide). It is then mixed in a vertical pug mill, which extrudes it in a continuous piece about 10″ (25.4 cm) square. From there it is pugged in a horizontal mill to a diameter of about 5″ (12.7 cm) and cut into lengths about 1 yd (1 m) long, then is cut with a wire device similar to an egg slicer, which eliminates weighing each piece of clay. Thrown ware is limited to pitchers and globular forms, demanding more skill than straight-sided pieces, which are pressed.

Throwing is done in a standing or semistanding position (arrived at by leaning on a board inclined slightly away from the wheel, to the right side). From two to six wheels may be run from one motor by means of a belt and slip-clutch arrangement, and throwing takes place at a constant, quite rapid, speed. (Most German potters were observed to pull cylinders with the palm of the right hand facing up.)

Decoration is usually done on bone-dry ware and consists primarily of designs painted in a commercially prepared cobalt slip by women or girls related to or employed by the potter. The traditional brush is made of pig bristles and is about as large as a pencil eraser.

Wares are once-fired, and are usually stacked without shelves. Clay wadding about 1 to 1½″ (2.5 to 6.7 cm) thick is rolled out, flattened, and then sprinkled with sand. The kiln is set by stacking larger pieces first and working on up in tiers, or "bungs," which are kept separated periodically by wadding, preventing the tiers from shifting and tipping. Flattened, doughnut-shaped wadding placed around the rims of some forms helps reduce the diameter of a larger supporting piece so that it is closer to the size of the base of the object it holds up. Fired clay wadding is discarded, often to be crushed and used to repair streets and roads. (The shoulder of the road from Meckenheim to Adendorf is built up in some places of brightly glazed clay fragments.)

German Salt Kilns

German firing methods are presently undergoing a transition. The older, horizontal-type kilns fired with wood or with combinations of fuel oil and wood, are rapidly disappearing and are being replaced with much smaller, manufactured, gas-burning models. In Adendorf, for example, there were 37 large wood-burning salt kilns in the 1940s; whereas in the summer of 1976 there were but six. The Ministerium (a government watchdog agency) encourages the use of the newer kilns, which cause less air pollution than wood-fueled furnaces. The cost of wood has also risen in recent years, and many younger potters simply do not care for the hard, time-consuming work necessitated by wood firing.

Traditional European kilns have been of the updraft variety, based on Roman designs. It is not known for certain when or how the Germans elongated the structure, but it is unique to the history of kiln design. Whereas the Chinese built elongated kilns on hillsides to provide adequate draft at the firemouths, the Germans designed lidded portholes in the arches of their structures—retaining the updraft principle but providing combustion space to the front of and beneath the ware chamber. (One ancient kiln preserved as part of a pottery museum in Höhr-Grenzhausen has the fire chamber beneath and to one side of the structure.) By manipulating the lids, which may number from 10 to more than 30, careful control of temperature increase and atmospheric variables can be maintained.

The traditional kilns observed in Adendorf were from 13 to 26 cu yd (10 to 20 cu m). One, at the pottery of Eugen Braun, was 17 cu yd (13 cu m) and held approximately 10,000 pieces. The firing lasted 50 to 60 hours and consumed about 1,000 gals (about 4,000 l) of fuel oil and 15.5 cu yd (12 cu m) of wood. One hundred ten pounds (50 kg) of salt was used in glazing. Much of the production in Adendorf is of *knienchen troven*, or rabbit dishes, about 10″ across and 3″ deep (25.4 and 7.6 cm). (Millions of rabbits are raised annually in Europe, and the dishes are used to feed and water them.) In addition, a variety of pitchers, drinking vessels, jugs, and crocks is produced.

The newer, more modern kilns are gaining wide acceptance. Most are approximately 100 cu ft (2.8 cu m) in

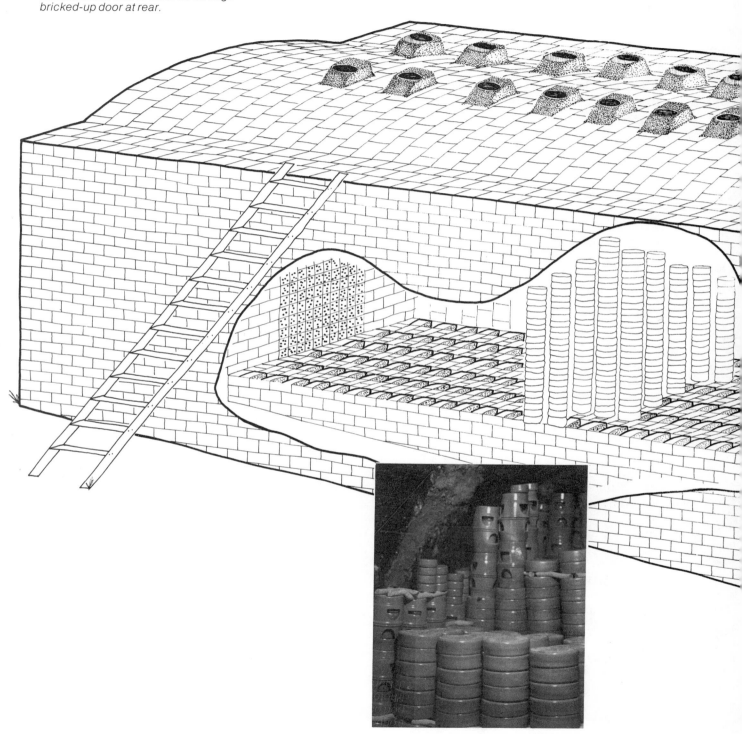

Traditional salt kiln. Indigenous to Germany, the updraft salt kiln was originally fired only with wood and more recently has been adapted to burn both fuel oil and wood. The kiln at the Eugen Braun Pottery in Adendorf contains 13 cubic meters and requires 4,500 liters of fuel oil and 12 cubic meters of wood to fire. The stacking space holds 10,000 production items and is entered through bricked-up door at rear.

Knienchen troven, or rabbit dishes, stacked in tiers nearly 8 feet (2.4 m) tall in a wood-fired salt kiln. They are fired to cone 5. Corzelius Pottery, Adendorf.

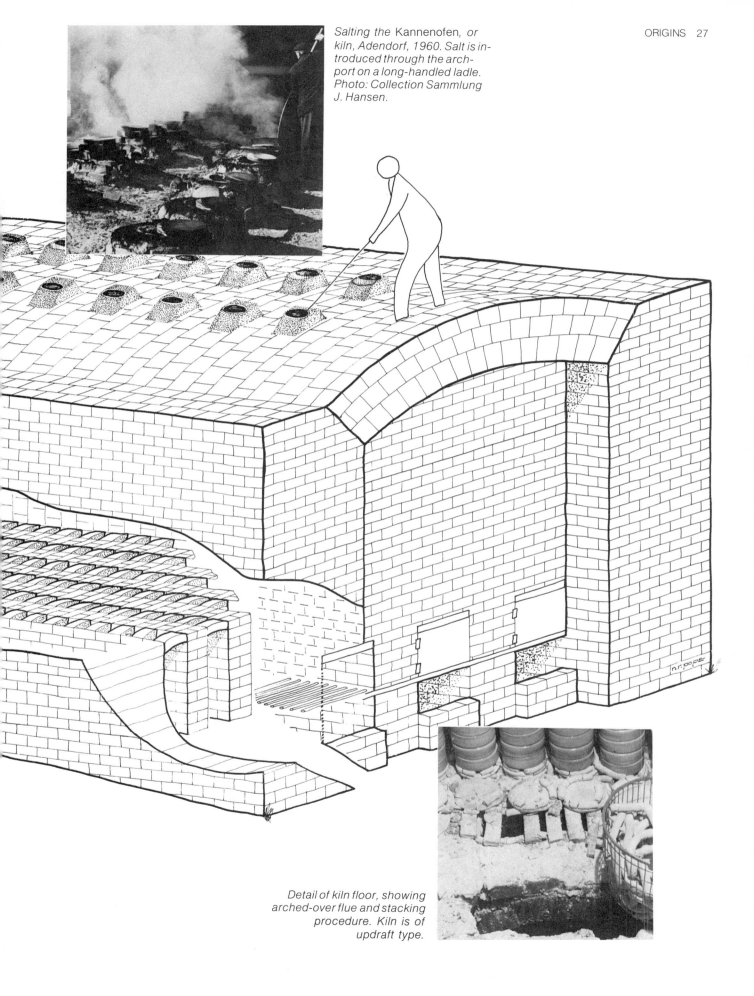

Salting the Kannenofen, or kiln, Adendorf, 1960. Salt is introduced through the arch-port on a long-handled ladle. Photo: Collection Sammlung J. Hansen.

Detail of kiln floor, showing arched-over flue and stacking procedure. Kiln is of updraft type.

*Karl Corzelius unloading his salt
kiln in Adendorf, May, 1976.*

Vase made by the father of Karl Corzelius, Adendorf, Germany. 16" (40.6 cm). 1920s. Bird and floral motifs were at one time so distinctively different that no other "signature" was necessary to identify the work. Cobalt slip on gray body, applied with pig-bristle brush.

capacity, with outside dimensions of perhaps 6 to 7 ft (1.8 to 2.2 m). The Corzelius kiln in Adendorf was fired with propane and forced air, entering from six burners, three on each side. Pilot lights with spark plugs were used, and a pyrometric temperature graph employed for each firing, to assure a high degree of quality control. The kiln is lined with alumina-coated insulating brick—replaced periodically—which is backed up by several layers of asbestos blanket or ceramic fiber insulation. The kiln has no chimney. Three ports about 9" by 4½" (22.9 by 11.4 cm) in the roof, located over the ware chambers, are used for salting and are kept partially closed during the firing, as is a 9" by 9" (22.9 by 22.9 cm) vent. Gas pressure is 7 kp/cm² (kilopascals per cu cm; approximately 1 psi), and cone 5 is fired flat, with cone 6 halfway over. A clear atmosphere is maintained throughout the firing, and cooling is rapid, by means of the forced-air blowers, when the burners are turned off.

The Corzelius kiln was under a high shed roof, and vapors were abundant during the salting. I asked an older employee if he knew of respiratory problems among those persons who had worked around salt kilns for many years. He said, "I have bronchial trouble. The only thing that relieves the condition is to breathe the vapors from the kiln." At the height of the firing he was observed standing in a dense cloud of fog, breathing deeply and loudly with great satisfaction. (This incident is submitted as an observation; not as advice.)

A German Salt Firm

The pottery of Hubert Neukirchen, of Adendorf, though now out of business, employed four men ("who never asked for a raise, but who knew as well as their employer when they should get one"), and the kiln, which held about 10,000 pieces, was fired an average of 21 to 22 times per year. One year 30 firings were held.

No cones were used in the firing observed at Braun's; rather, samples were taken out through a port and examined for signs of vitrification. Before the clay is vitrified completely, the broken piece, about 1" (2.5 cm) thick, shows a series of minute hairlike lines reaching to the center from the edges, but when the clay is completely vitrified, the lines are joined at the center and form a pattern radiating outward like wheel spokes. At that time salting commences, perhaps 2 hours after the oil has been shut off and wood is being used as fuel.

Stoking with wood is carried out rhythmically and

with great precision. One of the three fireboxes may receive eight pieces, each 1 yd by about 2" by 2" (1 m by about 5 by 5 cm) and the others six; and the sticks may be thrown halfway or very far in, depending on the judgment of the stoker. Flames and smoke rise 2 to 3 feet (.6 to 1m) from the ports, and standing on the arched roof of the kiln—about the size of a boxcar—one feels caught up in a process of great magnitude. Looking through the ports when the atmosphere has cleared, one can see down through the stacks of pots, a distance of about 10 ft (3m) or so. The kiln is remarkably quiet. (It occurred to me, standing on top of Herr Braun's kiln at the height of the firing, that all the salt kilns of the studio potteries in my home state of Pennsylvania would fit easily inside the one we were firing.) Someone breaks the spell by asking, "Where are all the rabbits?" There is laughter and a general easing up of work tensions.

The salting is carried out through the arch ports by Herr Braun and his son, who dress in heavy coats to insulate them from the heat and who wear damp towels across their faces, held in place by felt fedoras. In the vapor fog, they appear to be attending a series of small volcanos arranged in parallel lines. A long-handled ladle disperses about 2 cups (.48 l) of rock salt through each port, scattered directly over the pieces. Vaporization is instantaneous, and clouds envelop the top of the kiln, which is open to the sky, and dissipate quickly. The salting continues at ½ hour intervals for about 1½ hours, when draw trials from various parts of the kiln reveal a good glaze build-up. Bricks are used to seal up the fireboxes, the ports are left somewhat ajar, and beer is produced, dripping, from a well; cheese and sausage are passed around as darkness sets in. Herr Braun's son, who has just passed his final examinations in ceramics training, says the firing has gone well. His father, a sixth-generation potter, agrees.

Adendorf, where both the Braun and Corzelius potteries are located, is on the outskirts of Bonn, near Meckenheim. The village has a long and proud tradition of pottery-making (the main street is Topferstrasse, or "Potters' Street"), and one young potter, Joachim Hansen, has begun a collection of early pieces made in the village with the intention of housing them in a museum.

Development in England

Salt-glazed ware was imported from Germany in quantities during the 1600s and was presented to Elizabeth I

Wedding pot, inscribed and dated 1788.
Probably Brown Nottingham ware. Vic-
toria and Albert Museum, London.

Jug, inscribed ''Moses Froomes Livin in Chosely Parish, Nottingham, June ye 26th, 1759.'' 11'' (27.9 cm). Brown Nottingham ware. Victoria and Albert Museum, London.

as a high point of ceramic achievement. Its uniqueness and durability were highly prized and the earthenware potters in England and elsewhere on the Continent were eager to learn the secrets of the process. Some erroneous theories were advanced as to how salt glazing took place, including this one:

"About 1680, the method of GLAZING WITH SALT was suggested by an accident; and we give the names of the parties as delivered down by tradition. In this as in many other improvements in pottery, a close investigation of one subject has frequently reflected fresh light upon another; something altogether unexpected has been presented to notice; and not unfrequently from an incident comparatively trivial has resulted a discovery of paramount importance. At Stanely Farm, (a short mile from the small pottery of Mr. Palmer, at Bagnall, five miles east of Buslem) the servant of Mr. Joseph Yates, was boiling in an earthen vessel, a strong lixivium of common salt, to be used some way in curing pork; but during her temporary absence, the liquor effervesced, and some ran over the sides of the vessel, quickly causing them to become red hot; the muriatic acid decomposed the surface, and when cold, the sides were partially glazed. Mr. Palmer availed himself of the hint thus obtained, and commenced making a fresh sort—the common BROWNWARE of our day; and was soon followed by the manufacturers in Holden Lane, Green Head, and Brown Hills; the proximity of their situation to the Salt-Wyches, affording great facility for procuring the quantity of salt required for their purposes."[2]

Another, more believable, tale about the early days of salt glazing in England is this one:

"It is said that delft-ware potteries were preceded by a maker of salt-glazed stoneware—a German named Wrede or Read—and a curious story is told in connection with him and the difficulty he had in establishing his works. It appears that the people being surprised at the glaze he produced on his ware, and at the secrecy he endeavored to preserve regarding his pottery, noticing the dense clouds of vapour which every now and then arose from his kiln (caused, of course, by the throwing in of the salt through the fire holes when the ware arrived at a certain degree of heat) believed that he had called in supernatural aid, and that the fumes which ascended were caused by the visits of the devil. He was 'mobbed' by the people, his place injured, and he was forced to fly the town."[3]

Whiteware plates. About 1750. Staffordshire. Decorated with low-fire enamels. Bottom plate pierced with relief-molded texture. Victoria and Albert Museum, London.

(Left) Vase by Eliza Simmance (also bears initials of Rosina Brown, assistant). About 13½'' (34.3 cm) high. Late 19th century. Doulton ware. (Below) Vase by Eliza Simmance (also bears initials of Bessie Newbery, assistant). 10'' (25.4 cm) high. 1902. Doulton ware. Doulton Museum, London. Photo: Derek Rowe Ltd.

(Left: from left to right) Biscuit barrel, 1879; covered jar, 1892–99; and jug, 1879, by Hannah B. Barlow. Vase, 1883, by Florence E. Barlow. Doulton Museum, London. Photo: Brindley Muller Associates Ltd.

(Bottom left: clockwise from left) Slender-necked vase by Mark V. Marshall, about 10½'' (26.6 cm) high, late 19th century; vase by Mark V. Marshall, 11½'' (30 cm) high, early 20th century;

vase by Mary A. Thomson, about 10'' (25.4 cm) high, 1880; vase by Mary A. Thomson, 9½'' (24.1 cm) high, 1880 (bearing initials of J. Bowditch, assistant); bowl by Mark V. Marshall, 4'' (10.2 cm) high, late 19th century. Doulton Museum, London.

(Below) Jug by Arthur B. Barlow. 7¼'' (18.3 cm) high. 1874. Doulton ware. Doulton Museum, London.

Play Goers *by George Tinworth. 4½'' (11.4 cm) high. About 1886. Mouse group. Doulton Museum, London. Photo: Brindley Muller Associates Ltd.*

Spirit flask depicting Dr. Johnson, designed by Leslie Harradine. About 1912. Doulton ware. Doulton Museum, London. Photo: Brindley Muller Associates Ltd.

Votes for Women *inkwell. 3¼'' (8.2 cm) high. 1908. Doulton ware. Doulton Museum, London.*

John Dwight made his first stoneware in England, at his pottery in Fulham, outside London. In 1671 he was granted a patent for manufacturing salt-glazed stoneware in England, and a prosperous business developed soon afterwards. Where Dwight acquired his knowledge of salt glazing is unknown, but it may have been through German emigrants or by a visit to the Continent.

Shortly after Dwight's success, the Elers brothers began making their own salt-glazed work, thereby infringing on Dwight's patent. Dwight sued the Elers in 1693 and won the case. When his patent expired in 1699, the process became widespread and was centered around Staffordshire.

Salt-glazed stoneware continued to be produced at the Fulham works for more than 200 years, and large quantities of jugs, wine and beer bottles, and mugs were made, many differing only slightly from German prototypes from Frechen and, later, Grenzhausen.

Nottingham stoneware, characterized by red-brown metallic tints from iron-bearing clay washes, was first made in the early 1700s. By the end of the 18th century, wares made at Staffordshire from dense, semiporcelaineous clays were salt glazed, marking the first time translucent high-fired wares had been produced in this medium. Pieces were generally stamped out or molded and contrasted markedly with previous salt-glazed wares, which had been far less sophisticated.

About 1750 colored salt-glazed wares made their appearance from the pottery of William Littler, near Barslem, where blue slips were used. At about the same time overglaze enamels, similar to those from Kneussen, Bavaria, came into use. After 1775 transfer printing processes were applied to salt-glazed wares, and by the end of the century pierced basket designs as well as embossed and perforated bowls appeared, marking the decline of the art.

The salt-glazed wares produced at Lambeth by the Doulton potteries during the 19th century were truly unique. Doulton employed many artists who etched thrown or molded pieces, and produced a great variety of figurative three-dimensional work. Their factory facilities were made available to students from the Lambeth School of Art, resulting in "art pottery" that caught the public fancy. Due to the division of labor common during the 1880s and 1890s, no single potter was responsible for forming and decorating an object in its entirety.

Some of the Doulton kilns were enormous, having a seven- to fourteen-day firing and cooling cycle; and one such structure was known to the workmen as "St. Paul's" because of its size. It had a capacity of 29,000 cu ft (7,350 cu m), and each firing consumed about 30 tons (27,210 kg) of coal. Another was said to hold 40,000 ginger-beer bottles.

Development in the Northeast United States

Although earthenware is known to have been made in the Colonies as early as 1635 (by Philip Drinker of Charlestown, Massachusetts), excavations in Jamestown, Virginia, indicate that a crude form of earthenware was produced there between 1625 and 1650. In any case, by 1640 pieces lined with lead glaze were being made, and the earthenware tradition continued for about 200 years.

Stoneware was probably first produced in the 1720s. The earliest known piece, a jar made by Joseph Thiekson in New Jersey, is dated 1722, and the Duché family is recorded as having made stoneware in Philadelphia by at least 1730. One of the most successful potteries was that of William Crolius, born near Koblenz, Germany, in 1700, who came to New York in 1718. In 1726 he married Veronica Corselius, and the 1854 edition of D. T. Valentine's Manual of the City of New York mentions a "stoneware furnace" built in 1730 at the Corselius pottery. The name was apparently changed to the Crolius Pottery and operated in New York City until 1837. The Remmey pottery operated close to that of the Crolius family until 1820. A great deal of the potting activity in the Manhattan area took place near the banks of Collect Pond, long since filled in, around the present area from Reade to Duane Streets, west of Center Street.

Superior stoneware clays were found on Manhattan Island; near Huntington, Long Island; on Staten Island; and near Bayonne and Perth Amboy, New Jersey. They were transported by barge and sloop to nearby potteries and later taken up the Hudson River, where stoneware was made at Poughkeepsie and Albany by 1800. New Jersey clays were eagerly sought and eventually, in the mid-19th century, would be transported via canal across New York State and Pennsylvania as far as Canada, where they were the only available clays for making stoneware.

The development of New York State stoneware is documented by William C. Ketcham, Jr., in *Early Potters and Potteries of New York State* (see Bibliography). Dur-

(Right) Crock by William E. Warner, West Troy, N.Y. 13" x 13" (33 x 33 cm). 1829–70. Gray stoneware with blue design. Simplified handles evolved from earlier ones which stood out from the side of the crock. Courtesy of The New-York Historical Society, New York City.

Two-gallon jar with leaping deer. Made at White's Pottery, Utica, New York. About 1849–66. Munson-Williams-Proctor Museum of Art, Utica, New York.

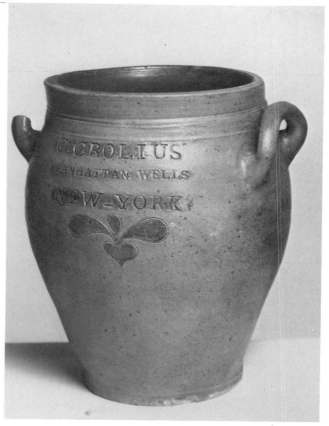

(Left) Batter jug and (right) jar by Clarkson Crolius Sr., Manhattan-Wells, N.Y. About 1798. Incised blue decoration. Batter jug courtesy of The New-York Historical Society, New York City; jar courtesy of The Brooklyn Museum, gift of Arthur W. Clement.

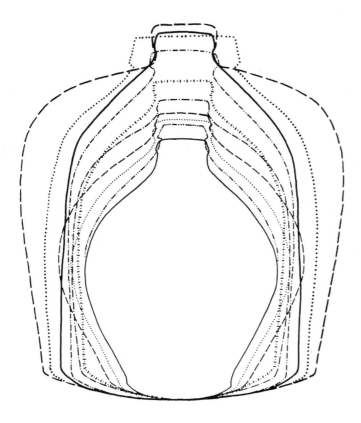

———————	Pre-1823
—··—···—··	1833-38
·················	1838-44
— — — — —	1844-47
—·—·—·—·	1844-47
·ı·ı·ı·ı·ı·ı·ı	1847-50
—··—··—··	1850-59
———————	1861-81
·················	1883-94
— — — — —	1886-94

Drawing showing the evolution of jug shapes at The Norton Kilns, Bennington, Vt., in the 19th century. From The Jug and Related Stoneware of Bennington *by Cornelius Osgood. Photo: Alex McBride.*

ing the 19th century, probably no state produced more salt-glazed stoneware than New York, whose Erie, Chemung, and Genesee Valley Canals were instrumental in providing transportation of clays and finished products. Ketcham lists 265 potteries making stoneware between approximately 1800 and 1900.

New England Stoneware

About 1740, Isaac Parker of Charlestown, Massachusetts, attempted to make stoneware, after having established himself as a successful earthenware potter, but met with failure. His wife and her brother-in-law attempted to carry on the business, had difficulty in dealing with the local clays, and turned to imported New Jersey clays; but the venture left them little profit and ended with their deaths in 1854.

The story of Grace Parker, as told by Lura Woodside Watkins in *Early New England Potters and Their Wares* (see Bibliography), is one of remarkable courage and persistence. Primarily because she considered stoneware to be "of public benefit" she carried on her husband's business in the face of great odds and personal tragedy. Even small gains in technical knowledge were extremely expensive and time-consuming. In one year three disastrous kiln firings—during the first, the kiln shrunk, settled, and collapsed—merely pointed out that their clay was inadequate for making stoneware, and that trial and error was the only available means of finding out. In her own words, such misfortunes were "no other than what have usually attended such as have enterprized things new and uncommon, howeyer beneficial soever they may be in time have proved to the Publick, or gainfull to the after-undertakers."[4]

The most famous New England potteries were those of Bennington, Vermont, begun by John Norton in 1793, when he built his first kiln for making earthenware. Between that year and 1894 members of the Norton family operated one of the most successful potteries in the history of North America. Their production of thrown stoneware (which began about 1815), most of which was salt glazed, has been documented and illustrated by Cornelius Osgood in his excellent book *The Jug and Related Stoneware of Bennington* (see Bibliography). It was at the Norton Potteries that many of the elaborate slip-trailed designs originated which were later to be recognized as examples of true folk art.

To be familiar with the changes in form which evolved

Jug by Daniel Goodale, Hartford, Conn. 15'' high, 10'' widest diam. (38.1 x 25.4 cm). 1818–30. Cobalt blue decoration. Courtesy of The Brooklyn Museum, gift of Arthur W. Clement.

Pitcher, probably made by John Rem-mey III, Philadelphia, Pa. 8'' (20.3 cm). 1815. Salt-glazed stoneware, cobalt blue and green decoration. Courtesy of The Brooklyn Museum.

Stoneware bank, Thomas Haig, Philadelphia, Pa. 7'' (17.8 cm). 1852. Gray salt glaze. Courtesy of The Brooklyn Museum, gift of Mrs. Huldah Cail Lorimer.

at the Norton potteries is to be made aware of subtly shifting attitudes toward pottery production that occurred elsewhere in the United States during the 19th century. Before 1823 jug forms were more or less onion-shaped, demanding a sense of proportion and design on the part of the potter that was no longer necessary by the end of the century, when straight-sided forms—easier to throw and stack—dominated production.

Pennsylvania Stoneware

Pennsylvania stoneware and earthenware was made by a large number of both English and German emigrant potters. Some made both earthenware and stoneware, but by and large stoneware producers had a competitve advantage and either forced the earthenware potters out of business or made it necessary for them to learn stoneware methods or move from the area. Some of the neighboring counties of Philadelphia, Bucks and Chester in particular, attracted potters during the early part of the 19th century; and, in the case of those in Chester County, many were Quakers and later abolitionists. They were known as "bluebird" potters because they farmed during the summer months and made their pots in the fall and winter, firing and selling them in early spring, about the time the bluebirds returned. As abolitionists, they were active in supporting the underground railroad; and many Chester County potters transported slaves or families of slaves in their huge wagons, hiding them among pots packed in straw. Runaway slaves were apt to seek freedom in the North as the spring advanced, and the kilns and woodpiles of these potters, located just north of the Mason-Dixon Line, no doubt were a welcome sign to many oppressed persons.

Earthenware clays were dug locally while stoneware clays came from Charlestown, Maryland, transported by wagon trains in the fall, between the harvest and the first frost. They were processed in a pug mill operated by a horse or mule walking in a circle and turning a central shaft, then kept indoors to prevent freezing. Kickwheels with flywheels were used, or the treadle-type "kick-and-paw" variety. Later, steam engines ran several wheels from a central power source with belts.

The pottery forms were straightforward, simple, and direct. Crocks, jugs, churns, pitchers, preserve jars, spittoons, and flowerpots were among the objects made. Decoration was simple, if any was used at all. Westward from the Philadelphia area, potteries devel-

oped in many towns. The Cowden and Wilcox pottery, located along the banks of the Pennsylvania Canal in Harrisburg, was one of the largest in the state. Salt-glazed stoneware made here was of exceptional quality and was often decorated with great vitality. Many small-town potteries flourished throughout the state in the mid-19th century, using local clays and producing simple wares for the community. A number of itinerant potters worked a season or two in one locale and moved to another. Quite likely, these were simply restless, often skilled, individuals who were reluctant to make the material commitment of staying in one place, which ownership of a pottery can entail. The foremost pottery west of the Alleghenies was S. R. Dillinger's, founded at New Geneva in 1854. The wares made here were similar to those produced by the James Hamilton pottery in Greensboro, each using stenciled decorations.

Most western Pennsylvania potteries had access to the Allegheny and Monongahela Rivers for transporting their wares, which were made from rather dark-burning clays. Some potters migrating west through Pennsylvania headed south and worked in the Waynesboro area. Most famous were members of the Bell family, makers of earthenware and stoneware, who moved south through Hagerstown, Maryland, and established themselves at various points in the Shenandoah Valley, where good clays and an expanding population provided opportunities for advancement.

The production of stoneware in Ohio and, later, in the midwestern states was begun by Samuel Sullivan in Zanesville around 1808. As knowledge of the excellent stoneware clays spread, potters moved into the state at a high rate; by 1870, Akron, the seat of Summit County, had 35 potteries and was known as "Stoneware City." The Ohio River Valley provided excellent clays, and the river itself transported the finished wares downstream where they were absorbed in ready markets by an expanding population.[5]

Southern Stoneware

The production of stoneware in the South has been documented by C. Malcolm Watkins and Ivor Noel Hume to have begun in the 1730s (*The Poor Potter of Yorktown*, see Bibliography). Salt-glazed wares, often fired in saggers, were made at Yorktown and Jamestown, Virginia, in the tidewater region. The pieces are almost entirely copies of English salt-glazed wares of the period. Stoneware tankards impressed with relief patterns were common products, along with jugs.

In 1774, a 35-year-old potter named Thomas Andrews left London to settle in North Carolina, about 15 miles (24 kilometers) from the present town of Seagrove, where he obtained a land grant and began making pottery. In so doing, he became one of the first of hundreds of potters to inhabit and work in the area of central North Carolina, where the abundant clays and wood for fuel have been good resources for a thriving ceramics production ever since.[6]

Unlike the northeastern United States, where earthenware potters were largely forced out of business or made to revise their way of working, earthenware and stoneware were made side by side, although as early as 1775 there was popular opposition to lead-glazed wares, known to be poisonous. Stoneware was generally favored.

It is believed that salt-glazed stoneware in the South came in with the development of the groundhog kiln. In any case, salt-glazed pieces from the Jugtown-Seagrove area are unique in a number of ways. Having been fired in groundhog kilns, one side of the pieces may be more heavily glazed than the other, since salt was thrown directly onto the ware. Wood ash and sodium combined to produce celadon tones in the glaze, possibly owing some of their color to the "lightered" or rich pine knots thrown into the kiln at the height of the firing to produce an intense heat. The resins in such wood, now rarely available, probably were responsible for reducing conditions which may have caused iron in the clay to diffuse into the glaze, coloring it green or amber. Some Southern clays were quite high in iron yet glazed better than one might expect, possibly because of their high flint content.

Cobalt was very sparingly in the South because it was expensive and the competition among potteries was not as severe as in the North. Blue decorated pieces were rarely made, except as commemorative objects or special items. Also, because some of the clay bodies fired to darker values, the contrast between the blue slip and light gray clay of, say, the New York State potteries was not so pronounced.

The tempo of work in the South was more deliberate, and since huge stoneware factories tended not to develop, the objects retain much of the strength of character through the 19th century that their northern counterparts lost. Perhaps because many of the pieces were made for local markets, a measure of integrity was maintained that might not have been otherwise. The designs themselves underwent fewer radical changes, since they were passed from one family member to another; the presence of an older potter in a shop probably had a steadying, if not controlling, influence on the children and apprentices who worked there.

By the 1920s, when the nation's population gravitated toward the cities, the need for certain salt-glazed objects such as churns passed on, and cheap glasswares had made jugs obsolete. The fountain pen was in wide use, eliminating the need for inkwells—the potter's standby. The Society of American Florists which favored mass-production methods over handthrowing, had standardized their sizes of flowerpots in the 1880s.

In the early part of the 20th century very little salt glazing was being done, apart from the industrial application of glazing sewer pipes, drain tiles, and building blocks—a step which has continued up to the present in some areas, although fewer companies use the method because of the relatively large amount of air pollution from the huge beehive kilns.

Pottery Procedures in 19th-century America

The bulk of salt-glazed stoneware production in North America occurred between 1800 and 1900. Whenever possible, potteries were located close to a source of good clay, which was dug and typically processed by a horse-operated pug mill. The ware was usually thrown, and the basic unit of measure was one gallon. A 5-pound ball of clay was used to make a gallon jug or crock, which sold at an average of 5¢ to 25¢ per gallon, depending on the pottery. An experienced potter was expected to produce 100 gallons per day.

According to Clinton Coffman, interviewed in 1963 at the age of 90, the Mt. Herman pottery, near Elkton, Virginia, employed three men who threw 100 crocks or jugs four days a week and fired on the fifth. Their kiln held about 1,200 gallons of ware and in a single season produced between 20,000 and 30,000 gallons of wares.[7]

Wedging the clay was often done by an apprentice or helper, and it was brought to the thrower weighed out in the proper-sized balls for the day's production. The pieces were slip glazed inside when leatherhard and were decorated quite rapidly, as a rule. Smaller pieces

(Left) Churn by J. D. Craven. 15⅜''
(39 cm). Mid-19th century. Gray
stoneware. Courtesy of The New
York Historical Society,
New York City.

(Bottom left) Six-gallon churn, maker
unknown. 19th century. Cobalt decoration depicts fish about to devour
shrimp. Courtesy Kinzle Antiques,
Duncansville, Pa. Photo: Alex
McBride.

(Bottom right) Six-gallon crock,
maker unknown. 19th century. Cobalt slip-trailed decoration. Courtesy
Kinzle's Antiques, Duncansville, Pa.
Photo: Alex McBride.

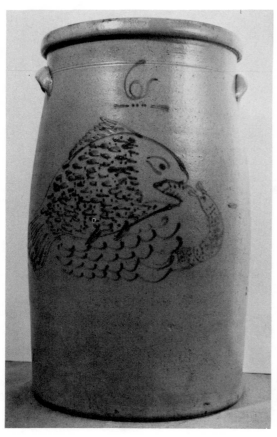

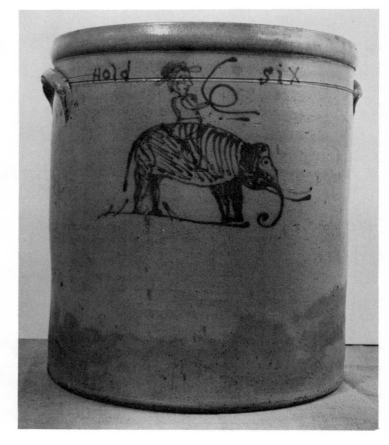

were usually coated entirely with Albany slip and placed within larger crocks, where they would not be exposed to the sodium vapors. The decoration of stoneware seems to have developed in proportion to competition, and few backcountry potteries decorated their wares elaborately, since they had a ready market for their work. In addition, the cost of obtaining materials was often prohibitive.

The element most used in painted and slip-trailed designs was a form of cobalt oxide called "powder blue," although ochre seems to have been used in the earliest Bennington wares. Sometimes cobalt oxide itself was applied as a wash, in which case the surface of the ware is usually a flat blue-black. To make the cobalt go further, it was often added to the slurry left from throwing. In the first case, a heavy coating of salt would be needed to produce a glassy blue surface, which was desirable, and in the second, depending on the body, the design was more apt to be slightly raised and smoother. The larger potteries seem to have used smalt—a type of frit made by combining feldspar or sodium carbonate with cobalt oxide and silica, then firing the mixture and pulverizing it to make the decorating medium. Smalt was produced commerically at East Haddam, Connecticut, in 1787. Albany slip, cobalt oxide, and throwing slurry may also have been used in combination. Decorating formulas must have been guarded very closely and were rarely written down.

Anyone who has examined 19th-century blue-decorated wares has noticed the great variation in slip formulations. A few of the potteries which consistently show a high degree of sophistication in slip composition and application are: the Norton pottery of Bennington, Vermont; White's, Utica and Binghamton, New York; and Cowden and Wilcox, Harrisburg, Pennsylvania. The New York State potteries generally seem to have produced the most outstanding blue-decorated wares, whose flowing lines were undoubtedly related to the widespread popularity of the Spencerian handwriting method.

Unfortunately, little research has been done about early kilns in America. Most were torn down and the bricks recycled when the potteries were closed around the turn of the century, but it is generally agreed that two types were used—the round updraft and the horizontal "groundhog" variety[8], which may have been an outgrowth of the English New Castle kiln at Jamestown.

The round kiln, about 8 to 12 ft (2.4 to 3.6 m) across and 6 to 8 ft (1.8 to 2.4 m) high, seems to have been in use throughout most of the Northeast. Usually two or more fireboxes, opposite each other, led to a series of partially arched-over flues under the floor. Wares were stacked in such a manner as to permit flames to circulate in updraft fashion. A series of ports was located in the crown of the kiln, which was arched over. The entire structure was held compact with heavy steel bands, boards being wedged behind them to take up the slack as the kiln aged. This arrangement helps explain why many larger crocks and jars are deformed: because of their size, they were used to support the stacks of pottery, and were closest to the intense heat of the fireboxes.

Firing was usually done with wood and took 2 or 3 days, including a long, gentle, drying fire. From two to three cords of wood were used, and as long as 6 days of cooling was necessary.

One of the few written records we have on pottery processes in 19th-century North America apparently was written by Nathan Clark, who operated potteries at Athens, Lyons, and Mt. Morris, New York. These were called "Rules for making and burning stoneware":

"1st. Let the wheelman be careful to have every piece run exactly true on the wheel. Make them of a kind precisely of the same height & width, have the ware turned light, handsome shape, smooth inside & outside, the bottom a suitable thickness, and a good top.

"2nd. Let it be handsomely handled & smoothly polished in the proper season.

"3rd. Let the ware when dry be carefully set in the loft washed and blued.

"4th. Let the plats [flat coils for setting] be well made. Kiln cleaned out and mended in complete order for setting.

"5th. Care must be taken to set the courses plum & one piece exactly over another.

"6th. Have your wood in good order, raise your fire progressively, neither to fast nor to slow, examine well & understand the management of your Kiln so as to heat all parts alike, be careful not to throw your wood in the arches to soon or do any other act that may have a tendency to retard the heat, when fit to glaze have your salt dry. Scatter it well in every part of your Kiln (during this act you must keep a full and clear blaze so as to accelerate the glazing and give the ware a bright gloss) stop it

*Form by Don Reitz, Wisconsin. 30''
(76.2 cm). Overspray of cobalt oxide
accented with iron glaze and frit.*

perfectly tight and in six days you may draw a good kiln of ware."[9]

Nathan Clark approached his work with genuine sensitivity for line and form. He valued expansion and increased productivity, but not at the expense of well-wrought forms. The jugs and jars which came from his shops are among the best-conceived, most well-crafted objects to be passed from one generation to another. Their potting successfully coordinates proportion, grace, and utility—qualities which fell by the way as pottery production became an industry toward the end of the 19th century.

Contemporary North American Salt Glazing

According to W. Atlee Barber: "It was reserved for a woman, however, to breathe the breath of artistic life into the body of American stoneware, and under her deft touch, guided by refined instinct and inventive genius, the old utilitarian forms were converted into new and graceful shapes, and the crude blue coloring, which served for ornamentation gave place to artistic designs in relief, always significant, harmonious and thoroughly appropriate. The honor of raising the humble manufacture of salt glazed ware in this country to a place beside the finer ceramic arts belongs to Mrs. S. S. Frackelton, formerly of Milwaukee, but now of Chicago. A fine example of her work is a large jar, now in the Museum collection, which was purchased at the Chicago Exposition in 1893. It is two and a half feet in height, of the ordinary grey color, supported by winged feline feet and ornamented with fruited olive branches in high relief and rich blue coloring."[10]

With the resurgence of interest in ceramics in the United States following World War II, virtually all aspects of the field fell under scrutiny as offering possibilities for creative exploitation. Among the students to whom salt glazing had a special appeal was Don Reitz at Alfred University, who became interested in high-fire techniques in the 1950s. The appeal of vapor glazing was for him in the way the glaze revealed, rather than obscured, surface decoration. Then, too, the drama of the firing procedure captured his imagination. He has, at this writing, probably been glazing with salt longer than any single individual in the North American ceramics resurgence, and the appeal the method has for him has been expressed many times in his personal work, in forms of considerable strength, surface interest, and originality. Don Reitz is to salt glazing what Paul Soldner is to raku: a force whose commitment to a particular mode of work has provided a source of inspiration for many ceramists.

The particular appeal of vapor glazing to a growing number of its practitioners seems to lie in the opportunities for combining one or more ambitions: (1) the desire to influence clay objects in a creative manner during the firing process (in conventional glazing procedures, the firing merely "fixes" the effects established prior to loading the kiln); (2) for some, vapor glazing is a trend away from the dominating interest in reduction-fixed stoneware which has become a kind of "bandwagon" approach to firing since World War II; (3) the appeal of individual discovery in a relatively uncharted area motivates certain individuals. ("Do I dare say this? Maybe another reason my salt glazing has taken an individual direction—in every way, including technically—is that I found virtually nothing written on the subject when I started doing it; only a sentence or two in various general ceramics texts"[11]); (4) the realization for some persons confronting the smorgasbord of techniques available to a clayworker today that vapor glazing represents a logical, direct means of surface treatment—essentially the same reason it was used so extensively by earlier potters; and (5) perhaps the most obvious reason is that vapor glazing is the only way to obtain fired pieces with such distinctive color and textured qualities.

CHAPTER TWO

INFORMATION ON CLAYS

Although a variety of clays will accept vapor glaze, few of them by themselves will meet the needs of most ceramists. In short, many clays will accept a salt glaze, but comparatively few are plastic enough for throwing, dense and vitreous enough at the desired temperature, and free from excessive shrinking and warping. Therefore, clay body formulation is usually necessary.

Some exceptions are the clays used for centuries by German potters which are particularly well suited for their use and would be welcomed enthusiastically by any ceramist working in stoneware. Fine-grained and exceptionally plastic, these clays, particularly those found in the Rhine Valley, are remarkably responsive without additives. They can be thrown or handbuilt with ease and fire to a rock-hard consistency. (At the Corzelius pottery in Adendorf, I saw pots which had been stacked lip to lip in the cone 5 firing being knocked apart with a hammer and falling a foot or more into a steel wheelbarrow with no cracking or chipping.) It is no accident that a thriving ceramics industry has grown up near the location of these abundant, excellent clays.

The North American counterpart to such clays was mined between the 1770s and 1890s near Amboy, New Jersey, and was shipped via canal to many of the 19th-century country potteries in the eastern United States. This clay was in such demand that it was used to make all of the salt-glazed pottery in Canada—being shipped there on canal barges—since there were no known Canadian stoneware clays available in the 1840s, when high-fire production began at St. Johns, Quebec.[1] (The growth of stoneware production in the northeastern United States closely parallels the development of canals. Nearly all major potteries were located near water transportation.) This New Jersey clay was very plastic and free from impurities and had excellent fired characteristics. Often it was mixed with locally occurring clays to make it go further. It ceased being mined around the turn of the century.

Many of the desirable qualities of a good clay can be found by prospecting for local clays, which are often surprisingly good, particularly in the eastern, southern, and central United States. Much of the clay used in the salt-glaze production at Jugtown Pottery in Seagrove, North Carolina, is dug locally, processed in a hammer mill, then pugged for use. The quality of such clays may make it well worth the effort to obtain them.

What Constitutes a Good Clay for Salt Glazing?

The major considerations—physical properties—have been dealt with above, but the basis for them lies in the chemical components of the clay. Before going into this aspect, however, it should be stressed that within rather liberal latitudes, most clays in common use by ceramists can be expected to accept sodium-vapor glaze when fired to a temperature sufficient to make the body mature.

Perhaps the best technical analysis of clays suitable for salt glazing appears in W. G. Lawrence's helpful book, *Ceramic Science for the Potter*. In the chapter "Salt Glazing," he lists many of the empirical requisites for good clay body formulation. The alumina-silica ratio is critical to the capacity of a given clay to accept a sodium-vapor glaze. Tests have shown that alumina-silica ratios of approximately 1:4 to 1:12.5 are best. Clay bodies high in kaolin ($Al_2 \cdot 2SiO_2 \cdot 2H_2O$) or talc ($3MgO \cdot 4SiO_2 \cdot 2H_2O$) do not form a good salt glaze because of an improper ratio.[2] Due to their high alumina content, kaolins do not salt well when used in high percentages in a clay body; but, as in the case of porcelain bodies, an abundance of flint and feldspar may compensate to restore the proper ratio, resulting in a body that glazes well. Magnesia, found in talc, helps promote salt glaze if approximately 1.5% is present, but causes a dulling of the glaze if over 3% is used. At times, however, the presence of alumina and magnesia tend to promote warm ochre and orange body flashing, which can be a handsome effect.

The iron content of clay to be vapor glazed is an important factor, too. Generally speaking, the lower the temperature at which salting takes place, the less will be the effect of iron, even in percentages as high as 6%–8%. At temperatures of approximately cone 10, however, as little as 1.5%–3% iron in the body may cause noticeable darkening in the value of the fired product. Iron, especially "free" iron—added as oxide or red clay to the body—has a tendency to produce "punky" salt-glazed wares when reduced, resulting in poor thermal-shock resistance. Mugs, teapots, and casseroles are apt to crack when they are subjected to heat. High-iron clays frequently tend to fire to a rather dead brown hue and thereby eliminate many of the more subtle surface characteristics possible. If it is necessary to use such clays, they should be fired in as much of an

Stoneware covered jar by Steve Howell, Kansas. 30'' x 10'' (76.2 x 25.4 cm). Hand-built and thrown sections combined. Sprayed with earthenware clay slip, ash glazes, and white slip. Fired to cone 10–11.

Covered jar with threaded lid by Sandra Johnstone, California. 33'' (83.8 cm). Salt glazed at cone 5.

(Below) Form by Sandra Johnstone, California. Salt glazed at cone 5.

(Bottom) Metamorphosis by Tom Suomalainen, North Carolina. 6'' (15.2 cm). 1976. Porcelain and brown high-calcium clays. Cone 6 oxidation, with propane and wood. Photo: Evon Streetman.

oxidizing atmosphere as possible and / or masked off with an opaque engobe (see Chapter 3).

The silica content of a clay, as mentioned, is critical to its capacity to accept salt glaze, and the addition of 5%–15% free silica (flint) to a clay or clay body may greatly improve glaze quality. Barringer points out a helpful correlation between iron-silica ratios: "A 1% reduction in iron oxide is the equivalent to the addition of 7.8% silica to a body maturing at 2206°F / 1210°C (cone 7) as far as brightness is concerned. A 1% reduction in alumina is equivalent to a 2.7% increase in silica at all temperatures."[3] He also found that salt and borax, when combined, produce a good glaze at temperatures as low as 1922°F / 1050°C (cone 04), and suggests that the addition of small amounts of soda ash or salt to the body (0.2%–0.4%) will sometimes improve the quality of the glaze. Titanium oxide in amounts of 1%–5% helps increase glaze brilliancy.

Clays which contain lime (calcium) in amounts above 3%, especially in combination with iron oxide, produce green to green-yellow glazes. Many 19th-century salt-glazed wares from the southern Appalachian region, especially around the Jugtown-Seagrove area, exhibit these qualities. The Auman Pottery Museum near Seagrove contains examples of such work.

To complicate matters, the composition of clays marketed under brand names may undergo variation from one year to the next, as many experienced clayworkers will attest. Although these variations are, in the words of one refractories technician, "not significant in the normal refractory usage nor within our control,"[4] they make a great deal of difference to anyone engaged in the creative use of clay. The simple fact that the composition of the earth varies even within a single clay pit may have considerable bearing on the outcome from one firing to another. In addition, clays are rarely mined for potters and sculptors, who may represent a rather small proportion of the total buyers of a given clay. As materials come under greater demand, clay qualities may change perceptibly. The chemical analyses of most commercially mined clays are available on request from the research centers of the companies concerned. They should be reread from time to time, since certain changes can be compensated for by the addition of new materials to the body.

An understanding of these basic principles and a willingness to conduct a few simple tests with clays in use

may affect the amount of salt or other vapor agent required to produce a glaze. For example, it was found that an addition of 10% more flint to a clay body (stated in parts) composed of:

35.0	North American fire clay
35.0	stoneware clay
15.0	ball clay
7.5	feldspar
7.5	flint

caused such an improvement to glaze build-up that the amount of salt used in glazing could be reduced by one-third.

Clay Body Formulation

As mentioned earlier in this chapter, most clay bodies will have to be formulated by the potter to suit his own forming and firing techniques.

Earthenware Range. Very little experimentation has been done with salt glazing at earthenware temperatures from cone 06–04, although Paul Soldner and others have often successfully incorporated sodium vapors as part of the raku process. At low temperatures also, a sodium-vapor transfer process has come into use. This method produces beautifully flashed surfaces as a result of firing objects in close contact with salt-soaked straw in the manner originated in Japan, where seaweed was used similarly. The organic matter burning away deposits a sodium film or sheen on the object, localizing a blush of color which can often be handsome.

Low-fire vapor glazing offers the attractive possibilities of lowered fuel costs and increased kiln life. Clay bodies should be formulated which are high in clays known to take salt glaze at the higher temperatures, such as Avery kaolin and Kentucky ball clay. Talc, a common ingredient in low-fire clay bodies, should be avoided, as it resists the build-up of glaze. The addition of a body frit helps ensure density. (See end of chapter for body formulas.)

Middle Range. While vapor glazing in the cone 04 range is possible, the middle temperature range from cone 1–5 provides more flexibility because nepheline syenite can be used as a body flux in place of a body frit, which can cause deflocculation and limpness in the clay. Fuel savings will be considerable if one fires at this temperature, since comparatively large units of heat are required between cones 6 and 10. Refractory wear is proportionate, and a kiln fired to cone 5 or 6 might reasonably be expected to last two or three times as long as one being fired consistently to cone 10. Most German salt-glaze kilns are fired in the cone 4–6 range, and there is a reason to believe that much early-American utilitarian stoneware reached approximately that temperature. (See end of chapter for body formulas.)

High-fire Bodies. The stoneware temperature from cone 6–14 is the range at which most salt glazing occurs, possibly because of the increased popularity of reduction-fired stoneware at art centers and college and university ceramics studios. During the 1960s, firing to cone 9 became virtually an automatic process in North American studios. This may be one way of explaining why little effort has been made to research vapor glazing in the lower temperature ranges.

There is no question of the simplicity of glazing in the higher temperature ranges. Slip glazes are easily employed, and the clays themselves are in a natural state of readiness to combine with the vaporous sodium, assuming their chemical composition warrants it. Common stoneware clays can be used to make up the largest part of the body, with ball clay being added for plasticity and fire clay for texture. Kaolins and sagger clays may be used to influence body colors and provide additional textural variation. Sand is frequently added to salt-glazed stoneware bodies, grog less so, largely because the silica in the sand can function as a glass-former in vapor glazing.

Commercially available clays, purchased moist and ready to use, vary so much in composition that each must be tested to determine its usefulness. However, those clays which fire in the range of cone 2–10 and have a relatively low iron content can be expected to do best.

Though it has often been said that "the best clay is the one I am most used to," there is no doubt that a variety of particle sizes helps meet the user's requirements by providing fine grains for the "flesh" and coarser ones for the "bones" of the body. (See end of chapter for body formulas.)

Porcelain. Working with temperatures of cone 9 and beyond is the only way to produce true porcelain, and often this type of clay responds especially well to vapor glazing. Many porcelain bodies are extraordinarily brilliant from having been salt fired. Colored engobes

may take on considerable depth, and the range of values possible either on bare clay or over slips or glazes is quite unreproducible. Most porcelains exhibit crazing when vapor glaze builds up to any appreciable depth.[5] Also, there is a tendency for the bases of some forms to chip away when removed from a shelf, particularly a shelf carrying an insufficient amount of wash under a piece that has not been wadded. (Porcelain and silicon carbide fuse readily in vapor-glaze firings.) Certain types of lids may glaze in place due to the vitreous nature of the clay and the vaporous condition in the kiln. (Those lids which overhang their juncture with the pot seem to do best, rather than ones which are directly inset into a lip.) Generally speaking, porcelain vapor-glazed surfaces are more active, or have the potential to be, than those of stoneware, because of the clay-glaze interaction taking place in the presence of abundant fluxes at high temperatures.

Occasionally, an effect known as "salmon flesh" develops on porcelain vapor-glazed objects, particularly beneath foot rims or where the clay has been protected from direct contact with sodium-bearing fumes. The pink-orange hues frequently accent a piece to advantage but are difficult to reproduce with any consistency. Porcelain fired in partially open saggers is apt to exhibit such tonality, because there seems to be a minimal accumulation responsible for the effect—the sodium barely affecting the surface of the clay at all. Such flashing is also sometimes induced by using monosodium glutamate, partly or wholly replacing other sources. Although porcelain slips applied over stoneware may respond similarly, stoneware clays are usually too dark to pick up this subtle effect.

In a kiln which tends wholly or in part to reduce, porcelain or white-burning stoneware clays can be fired advantageously, because frequently the effects of a reducing atmosphere produce colors of great depth and clarity over a white body, whereas the same colorants might be uniformly flat and lifeless over a dark body. (See end of chapter for body formulas.)

Throwing porcelain can be like trying to train a jellyfish to improve its posture. The clay body is composed of relatively nonplastic materials of approximately the same size and would seem to be all "flesh" and no "bones." There is no doubt that careful and patient preparation can improve any clay body, but this is especially true of porcelain. It should be mixed by whatever

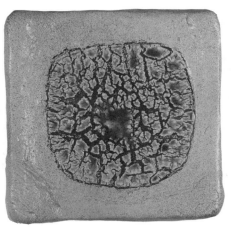

Handbuilt form by Bill Clark, Pennsylvania. 8'' x 6'' (20 x 15 cm). 1976. Heavily textured stoneware clay, scraped to create a visually rough surface, smooth to the touch. Photo: David Haas.

Form by Regis Brodie, New York State. 10'' (25.4 cm). 1974. Thrown, paddled, and handbuilt. Mishima technique with black slip. Salt fired to cone 9–10. Photo: Richard Linke.

Bottle by Regis Brodie, New York State. 14″ (35 cm). 1975. Thrown and hand-built white stoneware with inlaid porcelain and dark stoneware. Mishima technique with black engobe, Albany slip glaze inside and top neck of piece, salt fired to cone 9–10. Photo: Richard Linke.

Stoneware bowl by Don Pilcher, Illinois. 16″ wide (40.6 cm). 1976. Fine sand in the clay is accentuated against a dark background.

(Left) Gonzella and the Dinosaur by William Clark IV, Pennsylvania. Gonzella is 6'' (15 cm) tall, dinosaur is 3½'' (9 cm). Photo: David Haas.

(Bottom left) Syrup jug by Vernon Owens, Jugtown Pottery, North Carolina. 11½'' (29.1 cm) high. 1973. Courtesy Sam Sweezy.

Stoneware jar by Woodland Pottery, New York State. 1976. Incised and painted glaze decoration.

means available, 3 to 6 weeks ahead of time at the very least, using somewhat more water than is necessary to bring the mixture to the proper consistency for throwing. If possible, it should be kept in a large mass, such as on a pallet, under plastic, to age; and at least one-quarter of each batch should be slurry from previous use, although even 1 to 2 buckets will help start the bacterial activity that assists development of plasticity. Just prior to use, coils the size of an arm can be inverted, inchworm-fashion, to dry and be periodically wedged until a workable consistency has been reached. Warm clay ages faster than cold clay, but that which has frozen and thawed is remarkably improved.

Thrown porcelain forms of any grace and style must either be made from stiff, well-wedged clay or thrown thick and tooled. Well-thrown pots can have a vitality and spirit that stems from tension in the clay as it is coaxed toward the outer boundary of a given form. Tooled pots look tooled.

A clay or clay body can very easily be taken for granted if it functions well consistently, and the attitude of experienced ceramists towards their clay is a reflection of an approach to their work in general. Some seem to be restlessly in search of a clay which will perform in a manner consistent with their expectations of arriving at certain specific forms or surfaces. Others have used essentially the same clays for many years and the objects they make reflect a confidence stemming from familiarity with materials. Michael Cardew speaks of the clay of Abuja, Nigeria, as having a certain "tenacity."[6]

Still others could care less about their clays. When a participant in the Supermud Conference in Niagara Falls, New York, in October 1975, publicly asked California ceramist John Mason what kind of clay he used for his monumental projects, Mason immediately replied, "There's no magic in materials," and declined to elaborate.

Shoji Hamada has said: "You have to find the clay. Most clays will do as long as they have plasticity and will stand the heat of the kiln. Don't demand too much, don't look for the perfect clay. Natural clays have their own character, so do what the clay dictates—and perhaps add something for better quality, but it is best to use one clay only. The design owes everything to the clay's colour and substance. The best clays are the most difficult. I would rather use a low-grade clay with the hope of making good pots than first class clay and face the

Slab chest of drawers by Ian Gregory, England. 10½'' high (26.7 cm). 1976. Blue-green slip glaze; reduced iron body.

shame of making second class work with it. Mashiko clay is a low-grade clay, but I like its character and that is why I can manage well with it. It took me 15 years to learn to manage Mashiko clay. With first class clay 30 years would be needed. Once I found a very good clay near Nagoya. I had a small quantity of it sent to Mashiko, but I was never able to use it. It is still there in the corner. I would not even dare to make a sample with it."[7]

No shortcuts or plasticizers can compensate for carefully prepared clay, and anyone who has used such material can appreciately the time invested in its preparation. In Hamada's studio in Mashiko, Japan, a year's supply of clay is kept on hand in a mass about 10 ft high, 20 ft long, and 8 ft deep (about 3m by 6m by 2.4m). Shinsaku, Hamada's son, is quoted by Susan Peterson as saying, "Americans don't comprehend clay, the long stages of preparation necessary to make raw clay plastic and strong so that it won't crack in drying or firing. Clay must be processed for days, . . . and wedged by hand very much. Americans and the English just do not use enough 'arm.' Working the clay over and over by hand can't be duplicated by machine."[8]

Clay Body Formulas for Vapor Glazing

The following are clay bodies used by a variety of ceramists for several temperature ranges; they are given in parts by weight. All cone numbers refer to Orton Standard pyrometric cones.

Earthenware cone 06–04

Daniel Rhodes' Earthenware Body
25 Avery kaolin
25 ball clay
10 stoneware clay
15 frit
10 nepheline syenite
10 flint

Middle Range cone 2–6

Middle-range Body
40 ball clay
25 stoneware clay
10 plastic kaolin
15 nepheline syenite
10 flint

Stoneware cone 9–10

Rick St. John's Stoneware Body
50 Goldart (stoneware clay)
25 Tennessee ball clay
10 feldspar
 5 red clay

Sandra Johnstone's Stoneware Body
80 California fire clay:
    Cal clay
    Muddox mortar clay
    Lincoln 60, 400, or 800 clay
20 silica sand

Juniata Stoneware Body
100 fire clay
100 stoneware clay
 25–50 OM4 ball clay
 20 flint
 20 feldspar

Penland Stoneware Body
200 Pine Lake fire clay
150 Tennessee XX sagger clay
 20 feldspar
 50 Burns red clay

Betty Woodman's Stoneware Body
40 Lincoln fire clay
40 AP Green fire clay
10 Sutter clay
10 talc
10 feldspar
10 AP Green #30 grog

Betty Woodman's Dennis White Stoneware Body
35 Grolleg
15 Georgia kaolin
15 Tennessee XX sagger clay
12 Tennessee ball clay
10 flint
10 feldspar
 8 sand (optional)
 2 bentonite

Don Reitz's White Stoneware Body
25 kaolin
25 ball clay
25 flint
25 feldspar
15 fire clay
10 plastic vitrox

Porcelain cone 9 and up

Porcelain Body
55 Grolleg
25 flint
25 feldspar
 1–3 bentonite

Penland Avery Body
105 Avery kaolin
 60 feldspar
 60 ball clay
 45 flint
 30 Pyrophyllite

CHAPTER THREE

SLIPS AND GLAZES: THEIR COMPOSITION AND EFFECTS

Vapor glazes are normally transparent. Color is obtained by using one or more of four methods: (1) clay bodies colored with oxides or body stains; (2) slips, engobes, or glazes containing colorants applied to clay prior to firing; (3) colorants added to the salt or other vapor-glazing agent; (4) overglaze decoration and subsequent refiring.

Clay Body Stains

One of the first sources of stained clay body information was Paulus Berensohn's *Finding One's Way with Clay* (see Bibliography), which presents some excellent technical information for this method. Another contemporary ceramist who has used the method and arrived at specific colorants for vapor firing is Jane Peiser, represented in *The Penland School of Crafts Book of Pottery* (see Bibliography). Her work consists of a highly sophisticated method of handbuilding similar to the millefiore technique discovered by glassblowers. Many separately colored batches of clay are prepared and combined to produce surfaces of extraordinary graphic clarity. Her work is fired in an oxidizing atmosphere to cone 10. (See end of chapter for slip and glaze formulas.)

Engobes

A great deal has been written about engobes, since they have long been used to influence surface color in ceramics. Engobes are slips composed of natural or artificially colored earth materials used to coat clay bodies to change their color. (A slip is a clay or glaze suspended in water.)

Engobes have been used since ancient times by both primitive and sophisticated ceramists. In India, colored slip decoration dating from 5000 B.C. has been found in Harappa sites, and at later dates (4300 B.C.) in Egypt and Mesopotamia; slip-decorated ware in China has been dated as early as 3000 B.C. Neolithic pottery, dating from about 3000 B.C., decorated with red, black, and white slips—unglazed—has been found in Eastern Asia. Around the same time in Greece, the use of an engobe technique called terra sigillata come into use (see Chapter 4 on Surface Decoration).

Engobes can be thought of in painterly terms as grounds—surfaces on or through which additional decoration may take place. They are also vehicles for colorants. Engobes can be applied at any stage prior to firing, providing their composition is compatible with that of the

object—each must shrink at about the same rate.

The simplest engobes are made from the clay itself. In this way problems of the wet slip fitting properly are minimized and a wide range of color is possible when ceramic colorants such as oxides are added. Any body known to take vapor glaze well can be used, but porcelain bodies are especially effective since they tend to have a deeper interface—that juncture where clay and glaze mingle and are fused at maturing temperatures. Dry ingredients can be made up if colorants are to be added, or the slurry left from throwing can be used and applied to any piece made from the same clay body, as long as it is in the wet state and can therefore shrink compatibly.

Engobe formulas tend to have a longer firing range than most glazes and to be somewhat more compatible from one locale to another. Their compositions may vary widely, but the basic requirements depend on when the slip is applied and on its compatibility with the clay in use. Engobes used in the wet state usually contain about 50% raw clay, while those used on bone-dry work have about 30%–40%, and some bisque-ware engobes need only about 20%. The rule of thumb is that the more the piece must shrink, the more clay the engobe should contain. Some engobes will be found to work perfectly well with a given clay body, even though their theoretical composition may differ considerably from textbook examples. On the other hand, engobes which appear to be empirically "correct" may cause problems of one kind or another. Simple tests along the lines of those shown in Daniel Rhodes' *Clay and Glazes for the Potter* (see Bibliography) ought to be tried by anyone interested in arriving at original formulas designed for specific needs.

Engobes formulated for vapor glazing usually contain 15%–35% flint, since silica combines readily with vaporous sodium in the vitreous condition brought about by firing. The remainder of the ingredients can be kaolin, ball clay, nepheline syenite, and feldspar. Tin oxide or Zircopax can be used as an opacifier, and about 5% borax keeps the dried engobe from rubbing off when handling finished pieces (see end of chapter for engobe formulas).

Most engobes used by themselves will be transparent, translucent, or opaque, depending on several conditions, some of which are listed at the end of the chapter. The higher the concentration of flux (such as feldspar) and the lower the amount of refractory ingredients (such

Crock. 13¾'' (34.9 cm). Early 19th century. Incised designs on both sides. German-type handle. Courtesy of the New-York Historical Society, New York City.

(Right) Bread mixing and rising bowl by Ron Garfinkle, Maine. 7'' high x 12'' diam. (17.8 x 30.5 cm). 1975. Slip bands, fired to cone 10.

(Below right) Covered jar by Steve Howell, Kansas. 10'' x 13'' (25.4 x 33 cm). 1976. Handbuilt and thrown with handbuilt lid. Lightly sprayed on shoulder with earthenware clay slip. Fired to cone 10–11.

Covered jar by Barbara Sterne, Maryland. 7'' (17.8 cm). 1975. Stoneware once fired to cone 10, porcelain slip, incised decoration.

Ringkrug (ring-pitcher). 19'' (48 cm),
Westerwald. 1660. This monumental
piece is composed of three thrown
forms assembled and stamped then
painted with cobalt slip, which contrasts
vividly against the gray body. A pewter
lid conforms to the configuration of the
lip. Rheinisches Landesmuseum, Bonn.

as clays) suspended in the medium, the more nearly transparent the engobe will be, since the vapor glaze itself is clear and creates an even more watery surface.

Semiopaque engobes are particularly interesting since they offer the possibility of creating visually "deep" surfaces—those which may be no thicker than a page of this book, but which appear to consist of layers subtly differentiated, one from the other. Opaque slips are often monochromatic and mask off the clay body entirely.

What Are Some of the Phenomena of Engobes When Vapor-Fired? As the maturation temperature is reached, fluxes such as feldspar interact in the engobe and body to produce a chemical and physical bond, or interface. (If cooled at this point, the engobe would be as harsh and dry as an eggshell or very fine sandpaper.) Sodium vapors, liberated by the introduction of glazing agent, interact with the silica and other glass-forming ingredients in the engobe to form a very thin layer of glassy glaze. As the layer builds up through successive saltings, engobe colorants become diffused and suspended in the thickening glaze. Ingredients responsible for visual texture, such as titanium dioxide (used alone or as rutile, a combination of titanium and iron) or colemanite, as well as some of the coarser metallic compounds such as iron oxide or granular ilemanite, come under the influence of gravity, melt, and are drawn downwards on vertical surfaces or pool up in flat plates, bowls, or tiles.

This movement of suspended particles in the fluid glaze is responsible for "hare's-fur" streaks—highly prized by the Chinese stoneware potters of the Sung dynasty and sometimes obtained in vapor glazing. Hare's fur is an ephemeral effect, rather difficult to reproduce, which results from cooling the kiln at the time when a slip or glaze is in an intermediate stage of melting—somewhere between a mat and shiny surface. Temperature and atmosphere are critical to the development of this effect, which often forms as a glaze or engobe and heads toward a transparent state as the firing progresses. A reducing or partially reducing atmosphere seems to help develop this condition also.

Depending on whether an engobe-bearing object is located near an area of atmospheric turbulence or only partially contacts a direct flame, or is relatively protected from flame impingement, its surface may be flashed to transparency, blushed into a semiopaque condition, or simply glazed over to remain a visually shallow surface. All of these values may be present on a single piece, with transitional areas uniting them. Additional variables include:

(1) The presence or absence of reducible oxides in the clay body. In a reducing atmosphere these ingredients generally have a darkening effect on the engobe and may influence surface color and texture.

(2) The type of fuel used. Wood, for example, may cause more flame impingement with subsequent flashing than propane, with its shorter flame. Forced-air blowers may create more turbulence than a natural draft system.

(3) The length of the firing cycle. Most engobes, like most glazes, become transparent as they get hotter. The vaporous sodium may in turn eliminate signs of engobes by fluxing them to a glossy consistency during a prolonged firing.

(4) The thickness of the engobe and the degree to which it has been opacified. The thinner the application, the more nearly transparent the surface will be when it is fluxed by the vapor glaze.

(5) The method of application. Dipped and poured slips tend to be heavier than single, brushed applications.

(6) The concentration of colorants in the engobe. Metallic ingredients such as iron and cobalt may flux the engobe when used in sufficient quantity and fired to stoneware temperatures. A normally stiff engobe may be quite fluid if it contains 6%–10% iron oxide and is vapor glazed.

(7) Interaction with other slips, glazes, and frits. Glazes, coloring oxides, and frits are often applied over engobes and will naturally affect and be affected by prior surfaces beneath them. For example, a white slip may appear amber when seen through an iron-saturated slip which has been vapor glazed.

(8) The amount of vapor agent used during the firing. Each engobe has a range of effectiveness which depends on the thickness of the vapor glaze over it. At some point, the build-up of glaze may flux the engobe beyond evidence of having been used at all.

Experimentation alone will determine the possibilities inherent in any engobe. A given slip fired to cone 8 in an

Hanging vase by Jane Peiser, North Carolina. 6'' x 16'' (15.2 x 40.6 cm). Colored porcelain fired in salt to cone 10, overglaze fired at cone 017. Photo: Evon Streetman.

old kiln with heavy sodium build-up on the walls may appear much more fluid than if it had reached the same temperature in a new kiln, all other factors being equal.

Slip Glazes

Albany slip is one of the most versatile glazing substances available to ceramists. A naturally occurring clay which melts into a glaze around cone 8, Albany slip-type clay was used in the German Westerwald and by early American potters to line jugs, crocks, and jars, the interior surfaces of which would not be glazed by sodium vapors. Although this type of clay has been mined near Albany, New York, since the early 1800s, others similar to it can often be found through simple prospecting and testing of fired samples. At one time Michigan slip was mined commercially near Rowley. It has many of the characteristics of Albany slip and is but one example of the relatively wide distribution of such clays. Near Atacosa, Texas, Leon slip clay was used in the same manner; while another such clay was obtained near Elkhart, Indiana; and Richard Behrens reports having found a similar clay in the San Francisco area.

Albany slip contains roughly 38% clay substance, 13% feldspar, 28% flint, 15% magnesia, calcia, and potash, and about 6% iron. Although it matures in the cone 7–10 range, it can be used at cone 4 if fluxed with Gerstley borate, nepheline syenite, lithium carbonate, or iron oxide. Behrens' book, *Glaze Projects* (see Bibliography) is a helpful source of information on Albany slip-based glazes from cone 4–9, and a chapter on clay-based glazes in the same firing range is beneficial to ceramists working in vapor glaze and once-fired applications (see end of chapter for formulas).

Such slip glazes can often be applied to leatherhard clay by dipping, pouring, brushing, or spraying. Although the colors tend toward blacks and browns in straight reduction firing, vapor-glaze applications make lighter values possible with tones of amber and pale yellow, especially on porcelain and over white slips. Albany-base slips can be used as vehicles for colorants and can be applied to some clay bodies in the wet, leatherhard, bone-dry, or bisque state with equal success.

Glazes

Conventional glazes which mature at the same temperature at which salting takes place can be used in vapor-glaze firings, in which case the vapor glaze functions as

Covered jar by Rick St. John, Kansas.
High-kaolin clay body.

an overglaze. Glazes of varying characteristics should be tested for their compatibility with sodium vapors. Generally speaking, those highest in alumina, such as stony mat, high-clay varieties, will be less desirable, since sodium vapors will be resisted by them and tend to scum over the surfaces. Most feldspathic glazes, on the other hand, as well as the more fluid colemanite-base types, may work to advantage. Some deep bowls are particularly handsome when coated with a glaze known to function well in both conventional as well as vapor firings, since the interior upper areas will show the effects of the sodium while the lower interior may be quite beautiful in a different way from having been sheltered.

Soluble Colorants
Other methods of obtaining color in vapor firing involve the use of soluble colorants such as sulfates and nitrates. They can be used as additives to glazes, can be brushed or sprayed onto raw clay surfaces, or can be dissolved in water and used over engobes in amounts averaging from 5%–25%. Color from soluble sources is apt to have a hazy quality that lends itself to shading and air brushing. Soluble colorants may migrate through the walls of objects, influencing their interiors (see more information on Soluble Salts at end of chapter).

Colorants Added to Vapor-glazing Agent
The introduction of colorants simultaneously with the glazing agent has been tried and found to be a successful means of altering the color of the surface. It is reported by Sparkes and Gandy in 1896 that manganese dioxide was sometimes added to the salt to improve glaze color, and that lead in combination with salt assisted the fusibility of the glaze.[1] Parmalee mentions the practice of mixing crude oil with the salt to intensify color or make a dull black, probably by trapping carbon in the glaze.[2] (In Germany, where edible salt is highly taxed, industrial salt has crude oil added to it and is much cheaper. It is this form of salt which is used in glazing.) Lawrence cites the use of metallic zinc powder to produce green vapor-glazed brick.[3] In this case, zinc alone is used to produce the glaze. The metal volatilizes and forms a coating on the clay products. The color of such a glaze is apparently yellow, but combines with a blue body to produce a dark grayish blue-green color (in this case iron oxide in the body from 8%–18% and 6% alkalies favor such color development). Lenhauser reports that equal parts of salt and manganese chloride give a violet to red salt glaze.[4]

A contemporary potter, Tom Turner, has developed a method of producing copper-red glazes on light-burning bodies in a salt kiln by combining copper carbonate with the salt and maintaining a reducing atmosphere. In a 60 cut ft (1.7 cu m) kiln he uses 30 lbs (15 kgs) of rock salt into which has been mixed ½ lb (¼ kg) copper carbonate. He has also used copper sulfate to produce turquoise glazes in the same manner.[5]

While being an effective and even dramatic means of producing colored clay surfaces, this technique has the disadvantage of creating residual deposits of colorant in the fireboxes which may adversely affect later firings. Also, the entire stacking space in the kiln may be affected, which is not always desirable.

Refiring and Overglazes
Occasionally pieces fired in a reduction or oxidation atmosphere and found wanting can be refired in a salt kiln with some success: the opposite is also true. The quality of sodium-vapor glaze changes quite radically when refired in a conventional kiln, tending to flatten out, losing orange-peel effects and some definition of visual textures, but often bringing about a change of considerable merit.

Multiple firings can be carried out on previously glazed pieces, and have been since the French, Germans, and English began using overglaze enamels in the 17th century. The range of color available at, say, cone 04–06 is extremely wide, and one has the advantage of working with a dense, vitreous body made strong by having been previously fired to a high temperature. Commercially prepared glazes may be used as well as those compounded by the ceramist. Because of the vitreous nature of the surface being reglazed, several coats may be necessary, and are best brushed or sprayed on; some acrylic medium may be used to thicken the glaze. (It often helps to heat the pot before applying the second glaze coat.) Porcelain or light-burning bodies are best suited for this treatment, since they permit a wider range of transparent colored glazes to be used over them than do the darker bodies, which tend to dull subtle overglazes.

Low-fire luster glazes and decals which mature in the cone 019 range can be used on vapor-glazed objects. There may be some problem in adjusting decals to

Long-necked vase by Robert Winokur, Pennsylvania. 18'' x 10'' (45.7 x 25.4 cm). Stoneware with blue wood ash glaze over slips and engobes. Hare's fur streaks in midsection.

(Below) Covered jar by Peter Sohngen, Tennessee. 9'' (22.9 cm). Stoneware thrown and slipped, fired to cone 10.

(Bottom) Covered jar by John Glick, Michigan. 7'' (17.8 cm). 1974. Stoneware with soda ash vapor, fired to cone 10.

Bottle by Karen Karnes, New York State. 18'' (45.7 cm). 1976. Stoneware.

Pitcher with pewter lid. 10½'' (26 cm). 1680. Westerwald. Scratched and sprigged designs have been added to the leatherhard piece and negative spaces filled in with cobalt slip. Rhein- isches Landesmuseum, Bonn.

*Planter by Mary Nyburg, Maryland. 14''
(35.6 cm). Stoneware with titanium
dioxide wash with ash and Albany slip.
Photo: Tom DeLucca.*

strongly textured orange-peel surfaces, however, and if
one plans to employ this technique, the body can be
masked over with a smooth-firing engobe, or borax can
be added to the vapor-glaze agent (usually about
5%–10% is sufficient), which tends to promote a smooth
surface on the raw clay, relatively free from pitted texture.

Rich and intriguing surfaces can be had by fuming
pieces which have been glazed with commercial lusters
(see Chapter 8, Salt-firing Schedule). The pieces are
first fired to the maturing point of the clay and vapor
glazed, then lusters are applied, and, as the objects are
cooling from having been refired, stannous chloride or
other fuming agent is introduced into the kiln at the
proper time (see Chapter 8, Salt-firing Schedule). The
effects of an iridescent film over a silver or gold luster
can be very beautiful but demand close control over the
fuming process and good ventilation around the kiln.

**Engobe, Slip, and Glaze Formulas
for Vapor Glazing**

The following are engobes, slips, and glazes which have
worked to advantage for a number of ceramists in different regions. They are intended to be used as guidelines
and starting points and should be experimented with
freely. Unless otherwise indicated, formulas are given in
parts by weight. All cone numbers refer to Orton Standard pyrometric cones.

Engobes

Daniel Rhodes' Engobe cone 4–6
25 kaolin
25 ball clay
15 nepheline syenite
20 flint
 5 talc
 5 Zircopax
 5 borax

Tom Shafer's Engobe cone 2–10
30 nepheline syenite
20 flint
20 china clay
15 ball clay
 5 talc
 5 Zircopax
 5 borax

Craig's Base Engobe cone 8–10
35 flint
24 potash feldspar
20 ball clay
20 kaolin

Jessiman Base Engobe cone 8–10
45 ball clay
30 Potash feldspar
25 flint

Reitz Base Engobe cone 8–10
60 kaolin
15 feldspar
15 flint
10 ball clay

St. John's White Engobe cone 8–10
45 soda feldspar
23 Zircopax
16 flint
14 whiting
10 kaolin
 2 zinc oxide
 1 borax

Smith Base Engobe cone 8–10
30 potash feldspar
30 ball clay
20 flint
15 fire clay
 5 borax

Slips cone 6–10

87–95% Albany slip
13– 5% manganese dioxide
80–85% Albany slip
20–15% Cryolite
80–90% Albany slip
20–10% Gerstley borate
80–90% Albany slip
20–10% iron oxide

Slip Glazes cone 8–10

Daniel Rhodes' Boston Brown
60 Albany slip
25 Cornwall stone
10 whiting
 5 iron oxide

Bright Slip
40 Albany slip
34 Lepidolite
14 whiting
13 flint

Dark Slip
50 Albany slip
50 red earthenware clay

Fetter's Slip
54 red clay
23 whiting
15 potash feldspar
 7 ball clay
 3–8% rutile

Landshark Blue
16 Albany slip
 2 nepheline syenite
 1 cobalt carbonate

Red-brown
75–100 Albany slip
 5–15 rutile
 5–10 iron oxide
 5–10 potash feldspar

Stoneware Glazes cone 8–10

Val Cushing's Colemanite
50 potash feldspar
20 flint
15 Gerstley borate
10 whiting
 5 EPK kaolin
 4 rutile

Fake Ash
60 Albany slip
30 whiting
10 zinc oxide or
    barium carbonate

Jim Charanko's Ash
40 wood ash
20 Albany slip
15 feldspar
15 whiting

Rick St. John's Cannonball Salt Glaze Series cone 8–10

Blue
50 potash feldspar
20 flint
10 Wollastonite
 5 colemanite
 5 Tennessee ball clay
 4 red iron oxide
 1 cobalt oxide

Iron Green
53 potash feldspar
24 flint
12 whiting
 6 kaolin
 3 barium carbonate
 3 zinc oxide
 5 iron oxide

Iron Yellow
45 potash feldspar
23 flint
17 whiting
13 kaolin
 2 zinc oxide
 7 iron oxide

Copper Red
34 soda or potash feldspar
22 flint
15 zinc oxide
11 barium carbonate
 7 colemanite
 7 dolomite
 2 whiting
 2 tin oxide
 5 black copper oxide
   (omit for white)

Korman Yellow
40 soda feldspar
31 barium carbonate
12 dolomite
 9 kaolin
 9 flint
 6 iron oxide

Engobe and Glaze Colorants

Some commercial glaze and body stains make excellent engobe and vapor glaze colorants but may burn out at high temperatures. Consult manufacturer's specifications (see Materials Suppliers in the Appendix).

5–20% rutile: ochre, honey, pearl, opalescent, with texture

1–3% cobalt oxide: pale to bright blue; the strongest colorant

1–10% iron oxide: celadon, amber, honey, tan, brown, black; may flux

2–8% manganese dioxide: brown, purple, black; metallic values

3–15% titanium dioxide: ochre, pearly blue, opalescent, with texture

3–8% copper carbonate: green, red; to metallic values

3–8% ilmenite: yellow, tan, brown, with texture

Colorant Combinations for Engobes

2–6% rutile
1–3% cobalt   green

1–3% cobalt
1–3% iron or manganese dioxide   dark blue

1–1.5% chrome oxide
1–3% cobalt oxide   blue-green

3–5% iron oxide
2–3% manganese   black
1–3% cobalt

Jane Peiser's Porcelain Clay Body Stains

3% engobe stain # 555: turquoise (see Materials Suppliers in Appendix)	Standard Ceramics
6% body stain # 10776: pink	Ceramic Color and Chemical Co.
2.5% body stain # 1513: blue	Ceramic Color and Chemical Co.
6% body stain # 1347-6: gold	Ceramic Color and Chemical Co.
1% chrome oxide: green	Ceramic Color and Chemical Co.
7% iron chromate 1.5% cobalt oxide black 3% manganese dioxide	Ceramic Color and Chemical Co.
6–8% body stain # 6440: yellow	Mason Color and Chemical
7% body stain # 2426: warm brown	Mason Color and Chemical

Soluble Salts

The sulfates, chlorides, and nitrates of the standard ceramic colorants can be used in sodium-vapor firing. Usually one teaspoon to one tablespoon in a baby-food jar of water makes a workable solution. The sulfates of chromium, iron, nickel, and copper are especially useful for painted or sprayed decoration and can be used directly on clay surfaces, or under or over engobes and glazes. Because they appear very pale in solution, they can be stained with food coloring to assist in differentiating them during application.

CHAPTER FOUR

FORM AND SURFACE DECORATION

Vapor glazing was originally one of the simplest methods employed by ceramists. In eliminating the need to bisque fire and glaze each object, the process compressed the time between forming a piece from wet clay and having a finished product. The earliest German pieces bear few traces of decoration, but sprigged decoration, incising, and cobalt blue designs were common by the 1700s.

The range of methods and materials within reach of today's ceramist is more extensive than at any period in history, and contemporary objects are apt to show a sophisticated integration of a variety of forming and decorating techniques. This chapter will present several methods by which the forms and surfaces of clay objects take on certain characteristics as a result of decisions made by the ceramist.

It is not my intention to suggest that these methods be use in salt glazing alone, or that they are particularly unique; many have been employed for centuries. The fact remains, however, that when the decision to use vapor glazing is made, it may determine a sequence of events which begins with selection of clays and ends with unloading the kiln. The decorative process is an integrated aspect of this sequence, and a wide variety of possibilities are available.

Implications for Form

The form of any object must be seen as one characteristic of decoration, in the broad sense, if we define "decoration" by *Webster's* as "an arrangement in a work of art of purely sensory elements (as line, color, shape, texture) that stimulates pleasure without regard to meaning." Whether the form is rather rigidly determined, as in the case of cast, molded, or thrown objects, or freely constructed, the knowledge that it will be vapor glazed may have considerable bearing on the identity of the piece.

Vapor glaze tends to form on the outside of an object and to diminish in build-up inside, as the sides of a container, for example, mask the interior of the piece from contact with the sodium-bearing fumes in the kiln. This diminution of glaze often results in subtle gradations in surface values, ranging from rims which appear wet from having been heavily glazed, to the insides of cylinders or deep bowls, which may seem comparatively dry. Between these extremes may be seen effects very much like those of certain Bizen pieces, which exhibit subtle

light reflectance from having been barely glazed at all—the surface of the clay being visually heightened and emphasized rather than obscured by a heavy, glassy coating. (While lining an object with glaze is a way of insuring its being waterproof when fired, certain clay bodies, especially vitreous or near-vitreous porcelains, may be virtually waterproof without this precaution.)

The shoulders, rims, and exposed areas of pitchers, bottles, and jug-shaped objects may pick up more glaze than their feet, which tend to be sheltered from the sodium vapors. Convoluted forms or those stacked close to each other may show gradations of glazing from having certain portions of their surfaces shielded from the fumes. Unless one has a definite desire to coat an entire object with glaze (and this could be accomplished more effectively by conventional glazing methods) the characteristics of vapor glazing, with all its possible variations, ought to be capitalized on and seen as one of the unique aspects of the medium.

Much is to be gained from firing a vapor-glaze kiln with a load of objects lacking any glazes or slips, relying on variations in clay bodies, methods of construction of the pieces themselves, circulation "pathways" of vapors, and oxidation-reduction factors to determine the fired results. Particularly in a workshop situation, with a group of participants contributing a variety of forms, many variables can be documented and the kiln "understood" to a greater degree.

Alteration of Form

The transparency of salt glaze may be a determining factor in forming some objects. Textures as subtle as fingerprints will be revealed, often with startling clarity, by the glaze itself, and deeper ridges, depressions, and alterations to otherwise smooth surfaces can account for variations in glaze buildup. The use of ribs, particularly when throwing, can set the stage for a variety of textured glaze patterns on the compressed, smooth clay surface, especially if the body contains sand or granite chips.

Clay which has been beaten, folded, fluted, shaved, or stamped may offer advantageous surfaces for vapor glazing when used alone or in combination with other methods described later.

Addition to Form

The addition of sprigging, or pieces of clay applied to the surface of an object, can be especially effective in

*Ewer by the Rochester Folk Art Guild.
9¾'' x 6'' (25 x 15 cm). Wheel-thrown
stoneware, glazed with rock salt at cone
10 reduction.*

Color Gallery

The captions on this page refer to the following color gallery.

1. Bottle by Jack Troy, Pennsylvania. 20'' high, 52'' diam. (50.8, 132 cm). 1972. White and blue slips with rutile decoration. Coarse sand added to body. Collection: William Penn Museum, Harrisburg.

2. Unmarked pot with tulip design, Pennsylvania. Pot has a lot of bloating due to organic matter in clay. Courtesv Rick St. John.

3. Covered jar by Steve Howell, Kansas. 20'' (50.8 cm) high. High-kaolin body, sprayed earthenware clay slip.

4. Covered jar by Don Reitz, Wisconsin. 14'' (35.6 cm) high. Overspray of iron oxide and rutile.

5. Lidded container by Robert Winokur, Pennsylvania. 9½'' x 8½'' (24.1 x 21.6 cm). Stoneware, blue wood-ash glaze, slip, and engobes. Photo: Robert Winokur.

6. Handled pot and jug from La Borne, France. Pot, 10'' (25.4 cm); jug 15'' (38.1 cm) high. 19th century. Wood fired to cone 12; sodium-vapor flashing from cups of salt set in the kiln. Photo: Warren MacKenzie.

7. Form by Betty Woodman, Colorado. 30'' (76.2 cm). Porcelain with residual soda.

8. Vessel by Cynthia Bringle, North Carolina. 6½'' x 4¼'' (15.7 x 11.4 cm). Porcelain. Photo: Evon Streetman.

9. Double pot by Steve Dennis, Minnesota. 17'' (43.2 cm) high. 1976.

10. Two-gallon jug by Nathan Clark, Mt. Morris, New York. Prior to Civil War. Courtesy Rick St. John.

11. Mugs by Jack Troy, Pennsylvania. 7'' and 6'' (17.8 and 15.2 cm). Porcelain slip and rutile decoration. Photo: Wendy Holmes.

12. Vase by Jack Troy, Pennsylvania. 9'' (22.9 cm). Pictured prior to firing on page 111. Photo: Jack Troy.

13. Covered jar by Jack Troy, Pennsylvania. 7'' (17.8 cm). Porcelain with iron-saturated glaze, sagger fired.

14. Vase by Jack Troy, Pennsylvania. 14'' (35.6 cm), 1974. Porcelain slip with rutile. Photo: Jack Troy.

15. Teapot by Norm Schulman, Rhode Island. 12'' (30.5 cm) high. Fumed; slip painted and trailed; oversprayed with manganese sulfate solution. Photo: Norm Schulman.

16. Platter by Norm Schulman, Rhode Island. 20'' (50.8 cm) diam. Fumed; slip painted and trailed; oversprayed with manganese sulfate solution. Photo: Norm Schulman.

17. Plate by Myron Melnick, Minnesota. 21'' (53.3 cm) diam. Earthenware, fired to cone 04. Straw soaked in salt brine has burned away, leaving random patterns.

18. Vase by Myron Melnick, Minnesota. 20'' (50.8 cm) high. Stoneware, ''garbage'' fired, in presence of organic matter and salt brine on and near pot.

19. Covered jar by Don Reitz, Wisconsin. 14'' (35.6 cm) high. Stoneware with slip decoration, dry rubbed iron oxide and rutile with glaze and frit accents.

20. Bowl by John Glick, Michigan. 6'' (15.2 cm) diam. 1974. Glazed with ⅓ salt, ⅔ soda bicarbonate; partially glazed with celadon glaze, oxides for color. Wood/gas fired to cone 10.

21. Teapot by N. R. Pope, Montana. 8'' tall by 5½'' wide (20.3 by 14 cm). Slip-cast porcelain, pulled handle, tripod legs and hand-constructed stopper. Flashing created by rutile slips applied during construction. Each slip when fired creates a surface ranging from high glass to dull mat with some crystallization. Bisqued piece was lightly air brushed with cobalt carbonate and finally vapor glazed using bicarbonate of soda.

22. Big drinking vessel from Cologne. 9½'' (24.2 cm) high. About 1520. Hetjens Museum, Düsseldorf.

23. Covered pot by Tom Turner, Pennsylvania. Red glaze obtained through introduction of copper carbonate with salt.

24. Tea bowls by Jack Troy, Pennsylvania. 3½'' (8.9 cm). (Left) Landshark blue slip glaze (right) iron-saturated glaze, sagger fired. Photo: Jack Troy.

25. Vase by Jack Troy, Pennsylvania. 14'' (35.6 cm) high. Porcelain. Green and blue slips freely brushed. Photo: Jack Troy.

26. Earth Band V by Les Miley, Indiana. 17'' (43.2 cm) high. 1975. Fired to cone 10.

27. Platter by Don Reitz, Wisconsin. 20'' (50.8 cm) diam. Decorated with slips, incised line, and overspray of oxides.

28. Form containing river rocks by George Kokis, Oregon. 1976. Porcelain. Photo: Brad Miller.

29. Bowl by Don Reitz, Wisconsin. 12'' (30.5 cm). Stoneware. Overspray of iron, rutile, and cobalt oxide; glaze and frit accents.

30. Bowl by Norm Schulman, Rhode Island. 7'' (17.8 cm) diam. Fumed. Slip painted and trailed; oversprayed with manganese sulfate solution. Photo: Norm Schulman.

31. Covered jar by Cynthia Bringle, North Carolina. 15'' x 10½'' (38.1 x 26.6 cm). Photo: Evon Streetman.

1

2

3

4

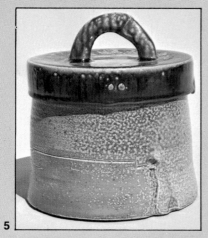

5

6

7

8

9

"I happen to like jugs. The broad shouldered ones thinning off toward the base appeal to me the most. I enjoy the touch of their cool bodies in summer and the uniform unevenness of their salt-glazed skin. I am old enough to remember as a boy the common use of the jug, to remember the admiration I had for a man who in an unconscious gesture could swing a jug into the crook of his arm and allow the mouth to settle gently against his own. I remember later how the liquid splashed over my face when I tried to swallow, and the laughter that followed. . . .

From Cornelius Osgood, Preface, *The Jug and Related Stoneware of Bennington, Charles E. Tuttle Company, Rutland, Vermont, 1971*

10

11

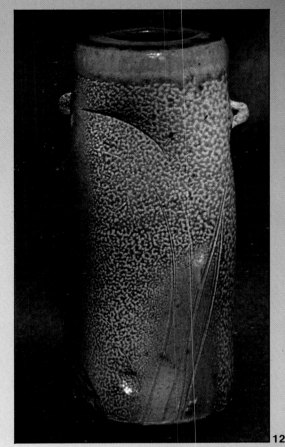

12

14

13

15

16

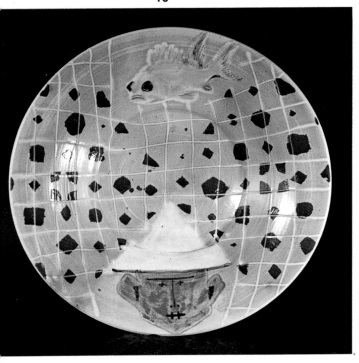

17

18

19

20

21

22

24

23

25

27

28

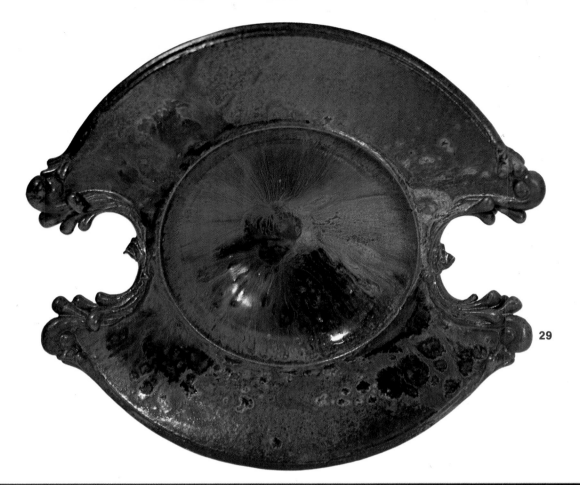

29

30

31

(Below) Extatic Chex *by Nancy Baldwin, New York State. 7'' x 3'' x 12'' (17.8 x 7.6 x 30.5 cm). 1975. Porcelain colored clay, blue and white. Photo: Leon Lewis.*

(Bottom) Box *by Nancy Baldwin, New York State. 4'' x 2'' x 5'' (10.2 x 5.1 x 12.7 cm). 1974. Stoneware with inlaid porcelain clay bodies, stained brown, green, gold, and white. Photo: Leon Lewis.*

the salt kiln, as it provides a raised surface and can accentuate details, particularly if clay of a contrasting color is used (see Chapter 2, Information on Clays).

Clay inlays are well adapted to vapor glazing, since their contrasting values show up with graphic clarity. (The method is described in detail in Paulus Berensohn's *Finding One's Way with Clay*; see Bibliography.) Body stains, oxide and carbonate forms of basic ceramic colorants such as chrome, cobalt, copper, iron, and rutile, as well as vanadium and manganese, are all valuable in this respect. (The Japanese *neriage* method of construction of varicolored clays is an adaptation.) Clay combination techniques became highly developed in 19th-century America, when "scroddled" wares were popular, often being composed of red and white or yellow earthenware clays which, when covered with a clear glaze, revealed colors woven together as in marble cake. Doorknobs still in use in many old homes were a common product of scroddled clays, as were vases and pitchers, which were frequently made in press molds.

Wet Slip Application

Slips, or engobes, are liquid clays. They are extremely useful to anyone working in ceramics, particularly in vapor glazing, for they make possible a wide range of surface values and can lend a quality difficult to achieve by other means. Chapter 3 described the composition of various slips and the following section of this chapter will deal with their uses.

Dipping, pouring, brushing, and trailing are four of the most common methods of applying slip to clay, and all can be done when objects are in any stage of development—wet, leatherhard, bone-dry, or bisque. A simple brushstroke of contrasting slip, for example, can be all that is necessary to create a focal point on a piece and establish a harmonious or contrasting relationship with the object that carries it. Whether deliberate or spontaneous, the act of applying wet slip decoration as the step following the forming of a piece lends an immediacy to the process and helps break down the time barrier which often gets between the clayworker and the object being made. Since vapor glazing offers the possibility of once-firing, the use of wet slip makes forming-decorating a unified act, leaving only drying and firing to complete a rhythmic cycle of work.

One method for throwing a series of pieces and slip decorating them as part of the same sequence would be

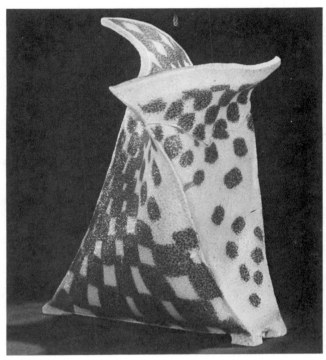

*(Below) Mug by Ron Garfinkle, Maine.
4″ x 3″ (10.2 x 7.6 cm). 1975. Ceramic decal;
double fired to cone 10 and cone 019.*

*(Bottom) Bowl by John Glick, Michigan.
6″ (15.2 cm) diam. 1974. Porcelain
glazed with 75% soda ash and 25% salt.
Celadon glaze altered by vapor. Fired to
cone 10 with wood and gas.*

to wedge the clay and put it and the tools necessary to the project close to the wheel. Keep buckets or jars of slip within reach, each containing a brush of an appropriate size for the scale of the objects to be made. As pieces are formed, they may be brought to completion with a rib, which compresses the clay, helps it stand up, and removes excess water from the surface. (Even relatively large thrown forms can be cut from the wheel and removed directly, since ribbed forms tend to be more tense than those thrown only with the fingers.)

When the form is judged to be complete, one of the slips could be used as a ground, masking off the clay body itself, and could be applied as the wheel turns by "banding" with the brush. If this first layer of slip is white, or porcelaneous, it may markedly influence subsequent slip applications by fluxing them and lending a translucent quality to otherwise opaque slips or glazes.

Brushes of various bristle characteristics should be used in this manner, for some of the most subtle and dramatic effects in ceramics have resulted from the use of freely applied slips, stated with a well-chosen brush. The Korean *hakeme* bowls come to mind, with their striated slip whirling out from the vortex, freezing the final rhythmic movement of their creation.

A typical pallet of engobes or slips for decorating may include a "base," or uncolored slip, as well as, say, blue and green variations deriving from the same formula. In addition, a rutile wash could be available as a color modifier.

For example, a 3,000 gram solution of Slip 1 is weighed out, dry-screened, and divided into three 1,000 gram portions. One part, Slip W, will be the white or base slip. Slip B will have added to it 20 grams of cobalt oxide, making a strong blue. Slip G will contain additions of 20 grams of cobalt oxide together with 60 grams of rutile, which in combination produce green. Water is then added to each slip in order to bring it to a consistency just a bit thicker than glaze—and the slip is then screened. Two to three tablespoons of rutile in a cup of water makes the wash.

Each of the above slips produces a rather brightly glazed surface (high in light reflectance) when vapor glazed. Rutile wash applied directly to clay often yields orange-gold or yellow tones, textured in relation to the body composition and the amount of glaze the body receives.

Since each slip contains the same basic ingredients,

Brushes

Few, if any, brushes are created specifically for ceramists, yet with only a little practice one can construct simple, serviceable brushes from materials as fine as various kinds of hair, up to coarse grasses such as broom-straw, all of which lend their characteristic imprints to applied wet slip and may furnish all an object needs for surface interest. Selected materials can be bound with thread or fine cord and the ends fused together with a waterproof epoxy-type glue, then secured in a clay, wood, or plastic handle. Such brushes often are useful for many years and require only a short time to make.

Slip 1

(based on porcelain clay body)

25 Kaolin
25 Ball clay
25 Feldspar
25 Flint

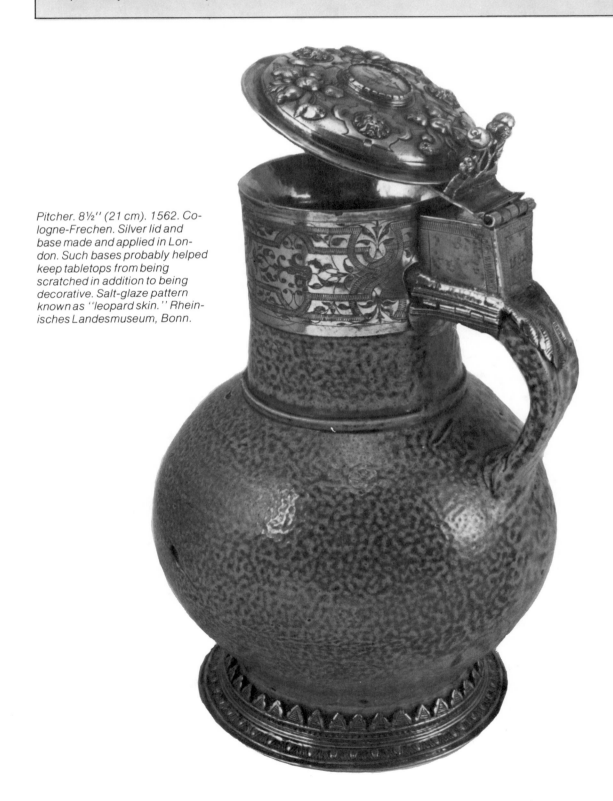

Pitcher. 8½'' (21 cm). 1562. Cologne-Frechen. Silver lid and base made and applied in London. Such bases probably helped keep tabletops from being scratched in addition to being decorative. Salt-glaze pattern known as ''leopard skin.'' Rheinisches Landesmuseum, Bonn.

(Left) Casserole by Ron Gallas, Pennsylvania. 4'' x 12'' (10.2 x 30.5 cm). 1976. The simple form is complemented by the subtle highlights in the variegated slip containing rutile.

(Below left) Goblets by Cynthia Bringle, North Carolina. 9'', 7'', and 8'' (22.9, 17.8, and 20.3 cm). Porcelain, thrown and altered. Photo: Evon Streetman.

Goblet by Barbara Sterne, Maryland. 7½'' (19 cm). 1976. Stoneware with porcelain slip containing 30% rutile and 3% copper carbonate applied to the upper portion. Foot banded in dark green Albany slip. Silica granules in the clay, perhaps in the form of sand, have become fluxed by sodium vapors, and appear as glassy windows in an opaque slip. Photo: Adam Sterne.

they are all compatible and may be used in combination to produce a palette of considerable variety. For example, an object could be coated with Slip W and Slip B applied over it to produce lighter values of blue with possible translucent areas where the first slip fluxes through the second, mitigating the effects of the cobalt. With the sequence reversed a surface could be created in which it appeared that one was looking through the base slip into the blue color layer.

Raw oxides or stains applied to the clay will bleed out into cover slips and will vary in tone more significantly than if the colorants were added to the slips themselves.

Slips can also be applied as distinct color bands or overlapped in any combination, with the rutile washed on to create yet another layer of color and/or texture. At any point, further contrast can be established by scraping through the layers down to the clay body. Rather swift application of the slips may be necessary to prevent weakening the freshly thrown form, particularly if it is thin. Extremely bulbous forms with small bases may collapse if slipped too soon and should set up until the clay is tense enough to support the weight of the additional water in the slips. Wax resist, applied either to the damp clay surface or later on top of leatherhard slips, can be another agent to incorporate in the process of building layers of color.

Sgrafitto, or carving through slip or wax resist, one of the most ancient and pleasing of ceramic effects, can be carried out in rather loose fashion at this point; more precise lines are best scratched during the leatherhard stage.

Combing, the creation of a pattern of parallel lines scratched directly into the clay or through slip exposing the body, can be carried out with considerable sensitivity while the slip is still damp. Combs and ribs can be useful in combining slips applied by brush, in patterns which can be arrived at by no other means. In a sense, one is caressing the freshly thrown piece, gathering the slip into thick and thin bands, which may after firing reveal depths of color and texture quite in keeping with the free manner in which they came about.

The above uses of slips, or engobes, have emphasized their application as grounds or bands of color, yet slip trailing in lines of various widths, using a bulb or syringe, is a method arrived at by early potters, one which reached its peak in mid-19th-century America.

Application on Leatherhard Ware

Many decorating techniques can be accomplished when the ware has dried to the leatherhard stage before firing.

Terra sigillata, a specialized form of slip, will be found to offer surface values of considerable richness, particularly to those who wish to employ precisely rendered sgraffito decorations.

To prepare terra sigillata, a clay known to salt glaze well is mixed with water to form a thin slurry and permitted to stand several days until the particles settle. Clear water will rise to the top of the container, and the heaviest particles will lie near the bottom. The water is siphoned off, and the top third of the remaining liquid is retained for the slip—the finest particles suspended in water. Such material can be dried, weighed, and colorants added, or it can be combined with sigillatas made from other clays to produce slips of extreme smoothness, very suitable for brushing or sgraffito. (Further information on preparing terra sigillata can be found in Joseph Veach Noble's *The Techniques of Painted Attic Pottery;* see Bibliography.)

Scraping of the clay surface during the leatherhard phase makes possible a variety of textures, depending on the tool used and the effect desired. Sharp-edged scrapers will reveal sand, grog, or other body additions, and the visibility of such granules will make them all the more accessible to sodium vapors. Each grain of sand or granite chip reacts with the vapor in a localized way, producing a "halo" of glaze around a white matrix of siliceous material which is so concentrated that it does not flux completely.

Conversely, coarse particles can be pressed into the object with smooth stones or shards of glazed pottery—and the surface smoothed further with a damp sponge. As the finer particles rise to the surface, presenting a uniform field to the vapors, the glazed effects will tend to be more uniform, with less orange-peel texture. Such smooth, semiburnished surfaces may stand in unanticipated contrast to glassy glazed areas, when fired according to methods described in Chapter 6, Special Effects of Setting Methods.

Paddling, either to change an object's shape or as a way of incorporating sand, grog, or bits of glass, ash, frits, or dry glazes into the surface, is best done during the leatherhard phase. Textured clay or wooden paddles are frequently used in this manner. Pottery forms particularly lend themselves to being gently dropped onto various surfaces and altered accordingly. Found or carved stamps are best applied at this stage.

Chattering, a technique used to remove portions of slip or to texture the body of an object, is carried out most often on the potter's wheel. A sharp tool made of spring steel, from ½ to 3″ (1.3 to 7.5 cm) wide, is held at an angle to a piece turning fairly fast on the wheel. A chattering pattern results, which can be controlled, with practice, to produce rather geometric, variously textured surface patterns in the later stages of the leatherhard state.

The application of dry oxides, glazes, or body stains or frits, feldspars, or vapor-resist materials such as flint, alumina hydrate, or whiting, can be carried out by dusting or spraying during this stage of drying.

Glazing for once-firing. The historical precedent for once-firing is very strong. Virtually no salt-glazed wares were ever bisque fired, and yet few persons once-fire today, possibly from force of habit. Slip glazes, especially those using 50% or more of Albany slip, can frequently be applied to leatherhard ware. The consistency of the slip seems to be quite crucial; experimenting is the best way to arrive at a proper match between the slip glaze and a particular clay body.

The different rates of shrinkage between slip and clay body often cause problems of cracking or crawling, and one way to avoid these is to calcine the dry slip to low red-heat before applying it. Another drawback to once-firing is the difficulty of removing unwanted glaze from greenware surfaces.

This is an area where several problems can arise, but the obvious savings in fuel and labor make once-firing an appealing aspect of vapor glazing.

Application on Bone-dry Ware

Clay objects in the bone-dry stage seem like skeletons—they are brittle, harsh-textured reminders of the pliant, supple materials they once were. Initial shrinkage has taken place, and the application of slips is risky because water absorption by the porous clay may result in cracking. Only raw materials with low shrinkage should be used in slips on bone-dry ware, and clay should be added in the calcined form. In contrast to slipping wet or leatherhard ware, brushes may skitter or drag across the

(Right) Handbuilt lidded box by Bill Clark, Pennsylvania. 14'' x 12'' (35.6 x 30.5 cm). 1976. The tight rectilinear form is relieved by a feeling of casualness in the lines created by the forming process. Photo: David Haas.

(Below) Thrown jar by John Ground, Pennsylvania. 20'' (50.8 cm). 1976. Sandy clay fired to cone 10; wood ash and cobalt slip.

Bottle by Don Pilcher, Illinois.
9″ (22.9 cm). 1976. Porcelain.

surfaces of greenware, due to the porosity of the clay.

Lightly spraying oxides or colorants on greenware works quite well if care is taken to avoid saturating the clay with moisture, which causes it to expand and crack. Spraying or painting colorants over stencils works well on greenware.

Sanding, brushing, and scraping all work well at this stage, and such objects as saw blades greatly accentuate the textures of the clay. Bodies heavy in sand or grog or other "toothy" materials can be given unusually tactile surfaces by sandblasting them in the bone-dry state, wearing away the finest particles, accentuating the coarser ones—the opposite effect from burnishing. A clay body darkened with iron or cobalt oxide could, for example, furnish a dark, rather dry ground for brilliant white vapor-glazed nodules, resulting from the addition of granite chips or coarse sand to the body—the counterpart, perhaps, to Shigaraki ware of Japan, made from clay containing naturally occurring feldspathic granules.

Application on Bisque Ware

Slips and glazes can of course be used on bisque ware, with wax resist, double dipping, and overglaze employed in the usual manner. (Any and all glazes formulated for the temperature range at which the ware is to be fired should be tested in the salt kiln as a matter of course, as mentioned in Chapter 3.)

One of the advantages of bisquing one's work is that slips and glazes used as liners adhere readily to the strong, porous surface of the ware, and one encounters fewer glaze-fit problems in firing.

Frits and feldspars, as well as ashes, dry glaze, or slip, can be rubbed, sifted, or sprayed on the surface of the ware without the problem of fragility encountered with bone-dry ware.

Marbleizing of slips and glazes is another method practiced by early ceramists which involves emulsions formed by mixing slips and glazes with oils or waxes instead of water. An oil-based slip is then floated on a water-base slip to produce textures on the ware similar to those found on the endpapers of certain 19th-century books. Considerable experimentation is necessary to produce this technique.

Conclusion

The above methods, as mentioned earlier, apply to a wide range of ceramic processes but are especially relevant to salt glazing. Given a lifetime and the motivation, any one technique could provide an adequate vehicle for meaningful personal expression. Decorating methods are best seen as tools, or as a vocabulary—as means toward ends which must be determined individually. A preoccupation with surface values at the expense of form seems pointless unless one wishes to disregard the three-dimensional possibliities of clay entirely.

Vapor glazing is no different from any other ceramic technique in the sense that it can be seen as a way to bring about a satisfying synthesis of form and surface.

The tendency too often, given the current availability of raw materials, is to confront the bewildering possibilities of surface manipulation like a hungry person at a smorgasbord, heaping the plate higher with tasty individual items at the risk of concocting a meal too varied and burdensome to be satisfying.

Perhaps trying various decorating techniques over a period of time is the best way to determine which will be most pertinent for meaningful, personally rewarding work.

CHAPTER FIVE
THE SALT KILN

Anyone with a serious interest in ceramics eventually builds at least one kiln. The proper time seems to occur for any number of reasons. To name but a few: one's work is victimized by another's firings, a work space of one's own becomes available, or an existing kiln needs to be rebuilt. The need for a kiln is often obvious and usually summons a great many random thoughts, each of which must be dealt with thoroughly, preferably over a period of time. Gradually a size and shape appropriate to one's needs begins to develop, and the methodical preparation, ordering of materials, hours of work, and revised planning add up to a structure which one comes to regard as an adversary in a quest for meaningful work. In the proper context, kiln building can be approached as an aspect of one's own work—such as a large project in handbuilding.

Any mortared kiln is a relatively permanent structure, and permanent structures need methodical yet flexible planning. Kilns begin with questions:

What is the anticipated scale of work to be fired? If sculptural forms are most frequently made, the need for shelves may be minimized. If smaller pottery forms predominate, shelf size and subsequent stacking space ought to be considered with regard to the size of the individual who will be loading the kiln most frequently. (Bending forward with heavy kiln shelves is certain to produce back strain and possible permanent injury and should be avoided whenever possible.)

What is the normal volume of work for the person or persons who will fill the kiln? This is a difficult question. A larger firing space than one is accustomed to frequently has a motivating effect on one's work capacity; yet a fine line separates this energetic attitude from being under a sentence—working to ''fill the kiln.'' In the making of pottery forms, a ''work-cycle'' approach will help, with perhaps enough ware being made for two firings back to back. Reloading the kiln before it cools completely saves considerable fuel.

What type of fuel will be used? Natural gas is convenient in that no storage is involved, but pressure may drop during peak demand periods. Unlike natural gas, bottled gas or propane must be bought prior to use and in northern regions may necessitate storage in a 1,000 gal (3,780 l) tank to prevent freezing the line when firing in cold weather. Fuel oil requires considerable bulk storage as well as a more complex burner system, usually dependent on electricity. Wood necessitates adequate storage space under a roof—some prefer to age-dry the fuel for at least one year prior to firing with it.

What materials are readily available? Cheap, locally available but short-lived bricks may be a sensible alternative to high-quality refractories shipped in at extravagant cost.

How often will the kiln be fired? It may be easier to justify cutting corners on a kiln used only occasionally, but extra investment in a structure on which one's livelihood depends would be advisable.

How much help, if any, will be available for construction? No more than two persons should be in charge, though several more helpers can be of assistance. In building most kilns, more than four persons can be a hindrance unless they are used to working together. With the right participants, a kiln building can have much of the excitement and flavor of a traditional barn raising.

These are some basic questions which will lead into more specific resolutions. Kilns are a specific form of architecture. Given the availability of current refractory products, many variations of size and methods of construction are within the range of anyone capable of defining his or her needs in rather specific terms.

Basic Considerations

After the initial questions have been answered satisfactorily, a practical assessment of location and materials must be taken.

Location. The location of any kiln deserves special consideration, and a salt kiln is no exception. The vast majority are located outdoors, where ventilation around the structure is at a maximum. Naturally, the prevailing climate has much to do with kiln location, and such activities as glazing are perhaps done best outdoors in the vicinity of a loading area. If conditions of space allocation warrant, a simple shed roof near the kiln housing shelves, furniture, kiln wash, cones, and glaze buckets is an asset. Kiln areas tend to become cluttered quickly, and to insure an efficient, safe work space, some sense of organization should be maintained. When a kiln has been unloaded, for example, and the pieces sorted and removed from the area, the warm kiln shelves can be washed, the furniture and door bricks arranged neatly,

Salt-glazed wares fired without shelves to cone 5. The interior of the kiln is washed to prevent vapor accumulation and to keep wares from sticking if they should touch the walls during the firing. Sandra Johnstone, California. Photo: Ben Zeitman.

Interior of old traditional German wood-fired salt kiln at the pottery museum of George and Steffi Peltner, Höhr-Grenzhausen. Arches were added prior to the final firings to keep the walls from collapsing inward. Large sagger in right foreground. Fine examples of traditional Westerwald cobalt slip decoration.

and order established for the next firing cycle.

One of the factors contributing to disorder around salt kilns is the relatively large number of objects of marginal success which may seem worth firing again, and later seem not to be worth the trouble. In addition, vapor glazing produces perhaps more "wasters" than other types of firing, and unless some provision is made for their disposal, they soon take up valuable space in the kiln area. Fired work should be "graded" vigorously and disposed of (sold, stored, or destroyed) as soon as possible.

If space is available, one should seriously consider setting aside a grave-sized area dug about 3 ft (1 m) deep solely for "wasters." Over the years, such a pit can serve as a reminder of former concerns and values. The instructional value of pot shards to archeologists is well known, but ceramists themselves stand to benefit as much if not more than by seeing slides of work, if they can sort through the fragments of their earlier efforts. I have always been reluctant to send shards to a common dump or landfill, especially after spending a hot afternoon in the swimming pool at the Jugtown Pottery where brightly glazed shards from earlier firings are embedded in the concrete. The Auman Pottery Museum in Seagrove, N.C., has salt-glazed shards found at old kiln sites embedded in the steps. Mosaics of all sorts could be fabricated from vapor-glazed fragments of pieces which are considered unsuccessful as a whole.

Proximity to the studio and the source of fuel are two very practical considerations concerned with kiln location. Ideally, a smooth, flat floor between the workroom (where objects are fabricated) and the kiln permits using wheeled carts or racks, cutting down on the number of miles walked in a studio during a year. Any reasonable amount of money spent for such racks, even though they may need to be custom built, will be a worthwhile investment, regardless of whether one is making "production" wares or large-scale sculptural forms. Clear, unobstructed walkways should be provided if objects are to be carried from one location to another.

Fuel sources are a factor in kiln location in that storage must be reasonably close to a transportation source. Propane and fuel oil tanks must be filled from bulk trucks, and wood is usually unloaded from vehicles which should drive to within reasonable distance of the storage area.

There should be adequate space around the kiln so that loading and firing take place in an uncongested area. Perhaps nothing contributes more to unnecessary feelings of tension and stress around kilns than working in cramped quarters. Too often, kiln location is one of the final decisions made in allocating studio space, whereas it should be one of the first. Although one must always make compromises with space, a *feeling* of spaciousness in a studio is a factor lying largely within the imagination of the individual. Many small work spaces appear commodious because of thoughtful organization of materials in a given area.

One should also consider the possibility that muscular fatigue attributed to loading kilns can be considerably reduced by planning and constructing serviceable equipment to simplify one of the most tedious and potentially injurious aspects of ceramics. If heavy kiln posts and shelves, door bricks and wadding clay can be kept at approximately waist height, lifting can be reduced and setting procedures speeded up considerably.

The presence in a studio of such articles as wheeled carts should not be considered to be "frills" but sensible necessities, the lack of which can result in strain, fatigue, and weariness—all counterproductive, energy-sapping bugaboos, too often thought to be the inevitable aspects of clayworking. Thoughtful preparation, with an eye towards avoiding unnecessary lifting around the kiln, should be part of planning any such space.

Regardless of the type of kiln one decides to build, a means of protecting it from the weather should be considered. Vapors are, of course, potentially hazardous in a tight space, therefore the enclosure of the kiln in a small building of any type seems unwise. A roof of transite or compressed asbestos fiber is one of the best materials, as it resists corrosion and is fireproof. Fiberglass roofing must be kept at a distance from any hot surface, as it may burn, melt, or deform. Such material should be cool to the touch at all stages of firing and cooling. Rolled aluminum roofing is an excellent weatherproofing agent and may be serviceable in sheet form draped over the kiln itself and does not necessitate additional supporting structure. Galvanized steel roofing may work well at first but will eventually corrode and need to be replaced fairly soon, unless kept at least 5 ft (1.5 m) above the installation or used with powerful ventilation.

The free passage of air around any vapor-glaze kiln is an absolute necessity. Even new and relatively tight furnaces may leak gases from the glazing process into the surrounding area, and definite precautions should be taken to prevent and cope with this occurrence. For this reason an outdoor location is suggested. Ventilation hoods and fans, if well designed, can make indoor-installation feasible, especially with at least 6 ft (1.8 m) of space between the top of the kiln and the ceiling. (Care should be taken not to vent fumes near open windows, air-conditioner intakes, or other potentially troublesome areas.) Doors and windows in any indoor location are necessary as well. There can hardly be too many.

Materials for Kiln Construction. From the very beginnings of salt glazing, the destructive potential of sodium vapors to brick must have been apparent. Even casual probings of the site of an old salt kiln will reveal brick fragments heavily glazed or spalled—deteriorated due to repeated subjection to high temperatures—to the point of being scarcely recognizable. Until comparatively recent times, salt glazing was considered a process that inevitably led to an extremely short life expectancy for the kiln. The comparatively large kilns of 19th-century North America may have resulted in part from the availability of brick that did not hold up as well as modern refractories, since the larger the structure, the fewer times it would be fired and the longer it would last. By comparison, smaller kilns fired rather frequently undergo considerable stress.

The longevity and durability of any kiln, then, depend on the quality of refractory material used in its construction. Traditionally, two schools of thought have prevailed in vapor-glaze kiln construction. The first and oldest favors letting the kiln self-destruct with age. As the bricks become glazed over, less salt may be necessary per firing, and there may be some validity to the feeling that old kilns, fired to the point of imminent collapse, produce some of the most highly prized objects.

The disadvantages to this method are several. Glaze accumulations may drip from the arch, marring objects below. Cracks in the walls may demand constant patching to prevent vaporous or liquid seepage and heat loss. Routine maintenance of bagwalls and fireboxes becomes more difficult as square and level surfaces give way to dense, organic-looking masses where heat is most intense. Glaze-fused bricks make dismantling and eventual disposal of refractories a difficult task.

The second theory is that the kiln interior should·be kept as free as possible from sodium vapor accumula-

tion. This can be done by using a high-alumina type of brick or castable refractory for any hot surface, and/or by regularly coating such areas with a sodium-repelling wash. Such treatments prolong the life of the kiln by preventing spalling. In light of high brick and fuel costs, this method seems most favorable.

To begin with, since the walls of the kiln are not continually being glazed, less sodium-bearing substance must be used per firing, since at best a small percentage of the liberated vapors ends up as glaze on the objects being fired. Increased longevity can be expected from shelves and posts due to their contact with fewer vapors. Coating the walls will have the effect of retaining or reflecting some of the radiant heat which might otherwise be absorbed by glazed walls and lost. While there may be a certain romantic attachment to the notion of crumbling kilns and magnificent fired results, the basis in fact is at best conjectural. Structurally, there is little question that, all factors being equal, unglazed kiln walls tend to crack less due to more even coefficients of expansion.

As the cost of refractory products increases, perhaps fewer kilns will be built according to the self-destruct plan, since the long-range expenses in terms of defective wares and replacement labor costs will almost certainly make the ''clean'' kiln a logical alternative.

Since the presence of alumina in any refractory material is a measure of its resistance to sodium vapors, bricks and castables for kiln construction should be of the high-alumina type, containing 50% or more of this material. The cost of such refractories increases with the amount of alumina, making the expense of a kiln comparatively high when refractories of more than approximately 70% alumina are used. There are many ways to pay for a kiln, however; and while the initial expense may seem high, long-term durability will almost certainly justify the purchase of the refractories with the highest alumina content one can afford. Fireboxes in particular are susceptible to spalling and breakdown and should be protected from the corrosive action of sodium by (1) regular washing with a 50/50 solution of kaolin and alumina hydrate; (2) using a castable refractory ''trough'' in the firebox where volatilization takes place; and (3) constructing the fireboxes with the highest-alumina-content material one can afford.

Mortars should be of the high-alumina type and may be purchased in wet or dry form. Unlike soft-brick installations, which may be stacked up loose, hard-brick kilns

are best laid up with a thin layer of mortar between each brick. Commercially prepared mortars can be used effectively, or fire clay can be mixed with water to the consistency where a hard firebrick will float in the bucket of the compound. Alumina hydrate and fine grog could be added to the fire clay as well in amounts of 10%–20% and 30%–50% respectively.

Kiln Types

The choice of kiln design is a personal matter. Several of the most common types in use—the sprung arch, the catenary arch, and the groundhog type—will be discussed, and some advantages and disadvantages of each mentioned. In addition, a more recent innovation, the castable, or poured refractory, type of kiln will be illustrated.[1]

The sprung arch kiln is in most frequent use in studio situations. It involves the construction of a box-type structure, roofed over by an arch "sprung" between steel supports—usually angle iron or channel iron—and connected by threaded steel rods or other external bracing. Kilns of this type work best if their dimensions are kept close to a basic box style—height, depth, and width being approximately equal.

The sprung arch kiln is constructed primarily of straight brick, and the stacking space is rectilinear.

As mentioned reviously, specific dimensions derive from individual needs. The size of shelf one feels most comfortable handling should relate to the entire kiln design. For example, the floor plan should be based on the configuration of shelves to be used.

The chief disadvantage of the sprung arch design is the angle iron and threaded steel rods which must be purchased to support the structure, and also the welding which may be necessary.

The catenary arch kiln is advantageous in that the arch is self-supporting and requires no external steel framework. There is some feeling that its design favors thorough penetration of vapors throughout the kiln, but this may be largely personal opinion. The aesthetic merits of such a kiln are attractive, as anyone who has built one will admit. Few experiences in kiln building rival the moment of pulling out the arch form from a catenary kiln, stepping back and looking through an arc composed of tons of bricks held together by a little mortar, good craftsmanship, and appropriate design.

Several disadvantages of catenary kilns are (1) Their tendency to "walk" or spread sideways makes a chan-

Shelves

Alumina shelves, particularly those 1″ (2.5 cm) or more in thickness work well in salt kilns if temperatures do not exceed cone 8. Above cone 8 silicon carbide shelves are best. Of these the "sandwich" type of shelf is superior, because its core is silicon carbide, while the top and bottom layers are alumina, bonded to the center. These shelves combine the strength of silicon carbide with the sodium-resisting qualities of alumina and do not require much maintenance. They are expensive.

The quality of silicon carbide shelves appears to vary a great deal, and some will be found tn last much longer than others, owing to fluctuations in materials and the temperatures at which they are fired.

nel-iron and steel-rod support necessary for the floor area of the kiln. (2) Stacking a catenary kiln can be irritating, at least until one becomes used to the peculiar interior space in the top third of the chamber. Ceramic forms frequently seem incompatible with the inverted-horseshoe space available toward the end of the loading. (3) Stacking the door may be a problem if loose bricks are used, since, again, the top third is of a curvilinear design. This section could be cast from high-alumina refractory material and inserted as a unit each time the door is stacked.

Interior Plan of the Kiln

The same floor plan holds true for both catenary and sprung arch kilns, the only difference being that as one builds up tiers of shelves in the catenary arch kiln, the remaining space becomes curvilinear, possibly necessitating the use of shelves of a shorter length.

In either case, construction details will differ little from a conventional kiln except in the following ways:

Ports. Salt ports or spyholes can be left in the walls of the kiln near the fireboxes to facilitate the introduction of sodium-bearing compounds.

Fireboxes. These are areas where the salt first liquifies, then volatilizes. They are liable to spalling and should be carefully attended to. One of the best methods to employ is that devised by Don Reitz, who shaped a trough-like device from A. P. Green's Mizzou Castable refractory.

Groundhog Kiln

The groundhog kiln is perhaps the only structure of its kind in North American ceramics and is indigenous to southern Appalachian potteries. Its burrowlike design necessitates crawling, groundhog-fashion, into the chamber to load and unload the wares. The arch is usually quite low—about 40″ (100 cm) in the center—and stacking is done on quartz pebbles, which are raked after each firing to loosen them. Quartz pebbles are sharply angular and make an ideal surface on which to place objects during a firing. They resist becoming glazed for as many as several dozen firings, are cheaply and easily replaced, and permit vapor glazing on the bottoms of objects, smoothly finishing surfaces customarily seen as rough and scratchy ones. In the production of pottery forms, wares may be stacked in saggers or on top of one another to use the available space. Shelves are rarely used in groundhog kilns since handling them in an enclosed space is difficult.

Groundhog kilns are unique in that salting takes place through the ports in the crown of the kiln. Vernon Owens at Jugtown told me that before cones came into use, one's judgment of the temperature of the kiln was determined partly by how long granulated salt remained on the shoulder of a jug before it melted and ran down the side. Jugtown wares are commonly salted at about cone 12, when granulated salt can be seen to hit a jug or jar and instantly trickle down the side of the form, while vaporizing immediately. Salt-fired wares from this type of kiln frequently exhibit signs of having been glazed from salt thrown onto the pieces from above. Apparently the practice of salting via the firebox was seldom if ever used in traditional Southern Appalachian pottery.

The chief drawback to a groundhog-type kiln is the space it occupies—often 5 to 6 ft wide, 12 ft or more long, and perhaps 4 ft high (1.5 to 1.8 m wide, 3.6 m long, and 1.2 m high). The excavation necessary for this construction may also be extensive. Earth walls usually hold the arch in place. The quarters in the kiln are cramped, and loading or unloading the wares is a tiring task (unloading the ware too soon, causing cracking, can never be done, since one must enter the kiln and remain fairly comfortable to be able to pass the pieces outside.)

In a sense, a kiln is a large pot or sculpture made to be fired again and again. Its construction is similar to that of a house, and it quite literally becomes a "home" where the identities of finished pieces of work are brought into being.

Castable Kiln

There are many references to early Middle Eastern and Oriental kilns, and illustrations of contemporary structures in Rhodes' *Kilns*, Sanders' *World of Japanese Ceramics*, and Leach's *Potter's Book*, see Bibliography. With a few general percentage compositions found in Norton's *Refractories* (New York: McGraw-Hill, 3rd. ed., 1949; pp. 290–98), the *Refractory Concrete Manual* published by the Universal Atlas Cement Company (New York, 1954), and with a grant from Westward Company of Detroit, combinations of raw clay, grog, and aggregates were fired to determine stability and thermal conductivity in 1969–70. A variety of inexpensive and easily available materials were used and proved to be efficient. In 1970–71 a series of six kilns were built using seven different mixtures that appeared to have similar firing characteristics of insulation fire brick. Of these kilns, the most thoroughly fired and tested was a series of four successive chambers, a climbing kiln that could be fired as a series of two and two or four in a row.

A catenary arch construction was chosen because of the ease of form-

continued

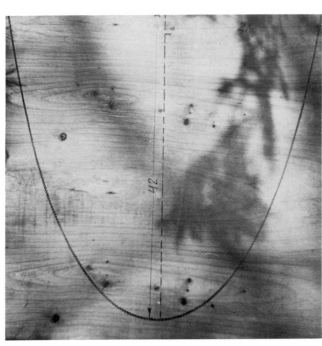

Hang chain to dimensions suitable for kiln size, based on factors in text, such as shelf size and types of objects to be fired.

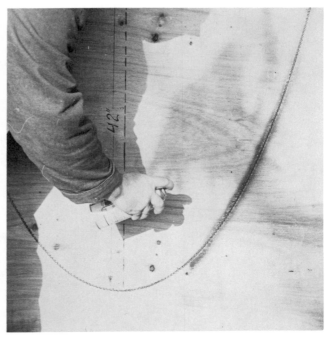

Spray hanging chain to form line on ¾'' (1.9 cm) exterior plywood.

(Above) First of three forms is cut out with saber saw.

(Right) Forms are lined up and side pieces attached.

ing and lack of iron needed to support the structure. The inner arch form, end plates, and side rails were made from ¾'' (1.9 cm) plywood, assembled on a base of the same composition as the arch, directly on the ground. Each succeeding chamber was built 8'' (20.3 cm) higher on cement blocks capped with the clay-grog-aggregate mixture 3½'' (8.9 cm) thick. The materials were mixed to stiff plastic consistency and

rammed into the form with 4x4s. About every 12'' (30.5 cm) a side rail would be added to the end plates. Casting was continuous and the walls brought up to within ⅔ the height of the arch. A piece of plastic was placed to separate the material, and casting continued to complete the arch. Monolithic castings tend to crack every 4 to 5 ft. (1.2 to 1.6 m), so it was thought best to indicate the most logical point in the curve sepa-

ration should take place. There was so little room to work behind of the kiln the back wall was cast in place. The side rails were cut 5'' (12.7 cm) longer than the arch form. Immediately after the arch was cast, the form was dropped and the side rails removed from the rear end plate, moved back and refastened. The arch form was withdrawn 2½'' (6.4 cm) leaving a space in the rear of the arch that was filled with castable.

Plywood surface presents smooth face for inner form when screwed in place.

Form completed up to steepest part of arch.

Form completed and end walls added, creating space for castable. Note reinforced end plates.

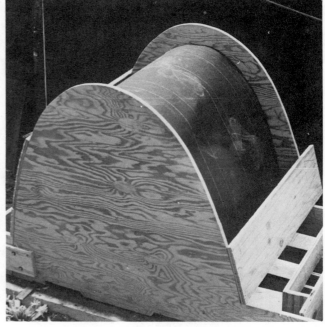

Inner form covered with tarpaper, to receive castable and permit easy separation.

This provided a keyed back wall in place. Total time for mixing and casting the arch and back wall was about 4 to 6 hours for two people. A simple form was made for casting the door which could also be used to cast the back. Doors and kiln parts should not be prefired above bisque temperature.

Castable Composition

The castable was composed of raw fire clay, coarse grog, and aggregates that included Vermiculite, sawdust, and wood chips, oat chaff screenings from the local elevator and crushed corn cobs, hammermilled bedding for livestock. A measure of Portland cement was added to the mixture to provide strength to the set and to allow completion of the kiln in one day. The same mixture was used for kilns one and two, a variation for kiln three and still another for kiln four. Kiln one had secondary insulation in the form of 1″ (2.5 cm) block and reached 1500° F (815° C) through 2″ (5.1 cm) of kiln wall and 1200° F. (648° C) through 4″ (10.2 cm). Kiln Two, without secondary insulation, measured 600–700–° F (315–372° C), at 2″ (5.1 cm) and 200° F (98° C) a quarter inch (.6 cm) in the outer surface. Kilns three and four were similar to kiln two.

continued

Basic arch on left has been tamped into place, the form dropped and moved up to create second chamber.

Arch showing compacted castable in place and smoothed over.

Double castable catenary kiln showing flue detail and arch form just prior to removal. Brick is cast into place over flue as lintel.

The chamber kilns measured 36″ x 36″ x 30″ (91.4 x 91.4 x 76.2 cm) deep and used about 1800–2000 lbs (810–900 kg) of material. Cost of the materials was about $65–70. Three sheets of 4x8 plywood were used for the forms and the same forms were used for all four kilns.

Following are the results of the various materials used.

Combustible aggregates

Vermiculite: Limited from 2.4 to 5.8% when introduced as the single combustible aggregate. The material tends to burn out or fuse at the upper limit, causing structural failure. It is efficient when introduced with other materials in 4 to 6% amounts.

Pearlite: Tends to fuse and combine with the clay, causing excessive shrinkage and vitrified body, thereby

losing its efficiency as an insulator.

Sawdust: Proves to be excellent insulation. It was used from 8 to 15% amounts and works well by itself. It is useful in combination with wood chips (to 15%) and oat chaff (6%). Coarse sawdust from a chain saw or sawmill is preferable to the fine material from a tablesaw.

Corncobs, crushed: Have proved to be an excellent binder and produced

(Above) Blocks 1″ (2.5 cm) thick have been pulled out from under the arch form, causing it to drop. It is now drawn out, leaving the arch as a free-standing structure.

(Right) Damp burlap permits castable refractory to dry and cure slowly.

(Above) Door form. Castable refractory when tamped into these segments will set up to become modules to seal end of kiln. Rear wall is cast in place.

(Right) Detail of flue prior to tying into chimney.

excellent insulation. The efficient useful addition ranges from 6.3 to 13%. In combination with other materials (vermiculite, sawdust, oat chaff) it works well from 2.5 to 10% amounts.

Oat chaff or screenings: From the local elevator; provided excellent insulation. When used alone its range was from 8 to 12%. Above 10% the structural quality of the sample suffered. It is excellent when used in combination with vermiculite, sawdust, and or works especially well with crushed cobs in 5.5 to 8.5% amounts.

The total percentage of combustible aggregate varied from 4.6 to 16.6% depending on the binding quality of the aggregate and the particle size and on the introduction of additional binders such as sodium silicate, bentonite, or cement. The average addition of all organic materials ranged 8 to 10%.

Clay or plastic materials

Raw fire clay: Additions varied from 27 to 50% without additional binders—32 to 45%, a wide variable, was the range of best insulation and binding qualities but depended on the type and particle size of the combustible aggregate. Air-floated bonding

continued

Finished flue tied to stack base; 55-gallon drum makes outer form; fiber drum used as inner form. Slit is for damper. Placing damper high helps assure heat staying in bottom of kiln.

Cast forms completed with doors in place.

Detail of burner pots at base of arch opposite flue.

Another castable kiln being built.

clay did not provide sufficient bonding when volume measures were used. When clay content fell below 32% the test bricks tended to crumble easily when prefired.

Refractory materials

Grog: Additions varied from 35 to 54.9%. The more grog, the less shrinkage. The most structurally sound wall will have only enough clay to fuse the refractory materials—38 to 53% grog depending on the type combustible aggregates and additional binders. The clay content can be lowered and the grog content increased with the used of cement.

Binders

Portland cement: Content was held between 7.8 and 10% in the test kilns. Some tests were allowed to cure normally before firing, others only briefly set before being installed in the wall of the test kiln. There appeared to be no difference in the thermal conductivity or in the ability of the mass to retain most of the structural quality of fired clay and the chemical bonding of cement.

Although Portland cement has only 2 to 3% alumina in relation to the calcium-silica ratio, the material did not soften or shrink measurably

Dry ingredients are mixed in foreground; water is added and they are shoveled into place.

Refractory is being tamped into place from top of open form.

Unscrewing sides of outer arch form; the structure has been completed and the inner arch form can be dropped and pulled out.

when fired to temperatures of 2300–2400°F (1160–1315°C). Refractory concretes, the calcium-alumina-silicates, have 35 to 40% alumina introduced in the raw mixture, sintered and ground so that on rehydration the refractory concrete is produced. In several tests a hydrated alumina was added to the mixture to approximate the composition of commercial mixtures. Further testing is being undertaken.

Bentonite and sodium silicate binders were not tested extensively. Stock molasses is another possibility for use with materials difficult to bind.

Additional chambers were built for the cost of the materials and the same forms were reused. The total capacity of the chambers is 64 cu ft (1.8 cu m), and total cost came to $295.00. Total hours for construct-

ing form 10 and for mixing and ramming 15 and raming were 15 per kiln. Grog proved to be the most expensive material used. If a source of crushed brick were available the cost per chamber would be cut in half. Combustible aggregate in test kilns is from 4.7 to 11.4%; clay content 34.5 to 43.8%; grog from 38.5 to 44.5%; and cement from 7.8 to 10%.

Hand ramming arch portion of kiln. Note ample air intakes under grates in combustion area.

The completed form showing wood stoke hole, ash drop, and flue detail.

Kiln interior. Note bag-wall arrangement which permits long flames from wood to climb up the arch and circulate through the wares before exiting at flues on left.

CHAPTER SIX

STACKING AND KILN SETTING

Salt kilns seem to produce quite variable results from one to the next, and even areas within a given kiln may produce different results according to stacking patterns and subsequent flame and vapor paths. Gaining knowledge of a single kiln begins with the first firing and continues throughout the life of the structure. The discoveries and understanding gained from this experience are a strong force in the intangible factor of identity which an individual feels in his or her work.

Stacking Considerations

Vapor glazing presents problems in setting and stacking kilns which are quite unlike those of any other ceramic technique. One must accept the knowledge that glaze-producing vapors in the kiln tend to coat any receptive surface, causing them to adhere to any other such surface. Objects readily stick to shelves. Bricks often glaze themselves together, and fireboxes may, in time, take on the appearance of volcanic residue. The accumulation of glaze on the arch of an old kiln may gather and drop like liquid epoxy glue onto objects below, fusing them, marring the finish, and only extremely rarely adding a feature to be admired in the least. Bits of mortar may drop from the arch onto objects below and be fused into place by the glaze, causing defects known as "nurds." Any firing can produce one or more of the above effects that sorely try the patience of any ceramist.

Shelves. The types and quality of shelves were dealt with in the previous chapter, but their use in salt kilns has been comparatively recent, following the discovery of the silicon carbide crystal in 1891 by the North American inventor Edward G. Acheson. Prior to that time, shelving material capable of withstanding load-bearing demands at high temperatures was either unreliable or unavailable. Traditionally, wares were stacked in columns lip to lip with clay tabs separating them, and "chocks" or handsqueezed coils of clay 2 to 5" (5 to 13 cm) long held the tiers of objects away from each other.

One cannot help admiring the patience and skill of the men and women of past centuries who stacked their bone-dry wares in tiers, often 8 ft (2.2 m) high, jugs and jars within larger crocks, using every available space. Each kiln stacking was a puzzle to solve with no means of support but the objects themselves. Working within such limitations naturally led to a certain standardization in the form and scale of work produced. By comparison, the use of kiln shelves grants today's ceramist the freedom to combine varieties of forms in any given firing.

Perhaps the transition between open stacking and the use of shelving can best be seen from the use of saggers in Germany and at Williamsburg, Virginia. Thrown cylinders customarily had four longitudinal sections removed to permit vapor flow to reach the mug within each one, eliminating the rough lips on the cups, which would have developed in stacking the shapes one on the other. (See also the section of Chapter 5 dealing with groundhog kilns for the use of quartz pebbles as an alternative stacking method.)

Kiln Setting

If one produces primarily sculptural vapor-glazed objects, stacking considerations will be minimal. On the other hand, plates, mugs, and small articles will necessitate the use of shelves and furniture. The scale of work may tend to grow, even unconsciously, as a way of avoiding the time and trouble implicit in loading a salt kiln, but if the hazards mentioned in the first part of this chapter are to be avoided painstaking care must be observed every step of the way when setting the kiln.

Before placing any objects in the kiln, a general cleaning of the interior and its shelves and furniture should be done as follows:

(1) Check the arch for loose mortar, and the walls for flakes or chips, and remove them, wearing leather gloves.

(2) Wearing goggles, vacuum or carefully sweep the floor and fireboxes clean of refractory chips.

(3) Coat the bagwalls and floor with kiln wash.

(4) Clean shelves and supports thoroughly, rubbing the bottoms of silicon carbide slabs with a piece of broken kiln shelf to dislodge loose glaze particles. Wash tops of shelves thoroughly—about a 1/16" (1.6 mm) thick layer of wash is best—and, if desired, apply a thin wash to shelf bottom.

(5) Make up wadding by wedging or squeezing alumina hydrate or dry kiln wash into plastic clay, or by dipping wads of plastic clay into the alumina or dry wash.

(6) Make up cone packs, draw trials, and kiln wash using one of these typical formulas:

A. 50% alumina hydrate

*Pitcher by John Glick, Michigan. 11''
(27.9 cm). 1974. Stoneware with soda-
ash vapor, partly wood ash glazed.
Fired to cone 10 with a combination of
wood and gas.*

(Right) Triptych by Tom Suomalainen, North Carolina. 10'' x 2'' x 8'' (25.4 x 5.1 x 20.3 cm). 1976. Stoneware sculpture, cone 9 reduction, salt fired. Photo: Evon Streetman.

(Below right) Covered jar by Karen Karnes, New York State. 12'' (30.5 cm). 1976. Stoneware, slip-banded.

50% kaolin or ball clay (the clay prevents settling in the bucket)

B. 100% alumina hydrate

C. 100% flint

D. 100% whiting

Unless the bases of objects are kept free from contact with silicon carbide, they will almost certainly fuse, so all shelf surfaces should be thoroughly washed. A further precaution would be to lightly wash the bottoms of the pieces to be fired, or to set them on small balls or tabs of clay dipped in alumina hydrate or dry kiln wash. Normally, three supports are enough for objects of moderate height with bases about 5'' (12.7 cm) wide, with more and larger tabs of clay being used as the scale increases. Ordinarily tabs should be about ¼'' (6.4 mm) thick to prevent them from exploding as the kiln gains temperature. These tabs can sometimes be reused if they are fairly uniform.

Bricks used as posts should be washed and clay wads coated with alumina placed between them and the shelves they support. These should be thin to prevent tipping of stacks of shelves.

Considerable experimenting may have to be done to find out which stacking patterns are best for the kiln being used, but generally vapor-glaze kilns are set or stacked more loosely than others in order to permit free passage of vapors. Shelves might be staggered in tiers to avoid a uniform spatial arrangement in the chamber, but generally, the smaller the kiln, the fewer considerations need to be taken along these lines.

Objects with fairly straight sides stacked close to each other may come from the kiln with fewer traces of glaze on the sides which bordered the pieces closest to them, and those in the center of clusters of pieces which shield them may show heavier glazing on their rims and tops than on the sides. Stacking too tightly around flues may decrease vapor circulation and prevent the kiln from drawing well.

Setting Methods and Special Effects

Objects fired together should be thought of as "family groups," each having a potential effect on the identity of one or more pieces. A small bottle bearing a stoneware glaze, for example, might be placed in a deep planter or covered jar and come from the kiln differing in no appreciable way from the effects of a reduction or oxidation firing. Squat pieces with large objects between them and the firebox may, by comparison, bear less vapor glaze, and single pieces in proximity to flame impingement may have "windward" and "leeward" sides relative to glaze accumulation. Oxidation-reduction patterns may be so regular in certain parts of the kiln as to make possible dramatic tonal shifts between objects or from one part of a piece to another.

Tall pieces placed within comparatively shorter ones will have glazed areas only on the exposed, uppermost portion; and flat, platelike objects fired on edge may act as partial shields to areas behind them (away from the fire source). As a general rule, the farther away from the firebox, the less dramatic will be the effect caused by grouping.

Blushing—the tendency of specific gas-borne vapors to affect objects they contact—probably occurs in all firings, but it can be utilized to advantage, particularly in vapor-glaze firings. Vapor dispersion during firing makes the grouping of objects a means of obtaining blushing. If, for example, a porcelain piece is placed near an object or objects bearing cobalt—as stains, slip, or glaze additives—it may exhibit delicate blue areas after firing, from the transmutation of cobalt via the sodium vapors. The same is true of stoneware, but to a less obvious degree, because the darker clay tones may obscure the ephemeral effects of the blushing oxides. Cobalt carbonate may be painted on bricks or bagwalls with similar results, and soluble colorants such as the sulfates and chlorides may be used in the same way.

Firing in Saggers. Saggers were originally clay containers used to protect ware from flame impingement, but flashing—color or textural shifts on objects which document flame patterns—can be manipulated with the use of saggers to produce effects of considerable beauty. These can be similar in some regards to Bizen wares—highly prized for their irregularities and fire-testimony markings. Using saggers can open up an entirely different way of relating to the firing process.

One of the simplest ways to make saggers is to throw or handbuild a series of unrefined cylindrical forms from rather coarse clay, with walls about ½'' (1.3 cm) or more thick. Some may be made to the same diameter, enabling them to be stacked in various combinations—lip to foot, etc. They could, for example, be cut directly from the wheel and set aside. When firm, holes of various sizes

(Left) Going By *by Bill Clark, Pennsylvania. 12⅜″ x 7¾″ x 1⅝″ (31.5 x 19.5 x 4.5 cm). Handbuilt stoneware. Photo: David Haas.*

(Below left) Form *by John Jessiman, New York State. 39″ high x 20″ diam. (99 x 50.8 cm). Reduction fired to cone 10, rutile slip. Photo: Douglas Long.*

(Below right) Storage jar with turned yew handle *by Ian Gregory, England, 16″ (40.6 cm) high. 1976. Orange-yellow slip with reduced river mud and ash glaze fired to cone 9.*

Sagger and vase. The open area has admitted sodium vapors to a portion of the pot while the solid portion has shielded the piece creating surface variation from dry to glossy. Photo: Alex McBride.

and shapes may be cut through the walls. The more holes, the more sodium vapors will enter and glaze the object within. In a sagger about 5″ high and 5″ wide (12.7 cm high and wide), four holes about 2″ wide by 3″ high (5 cm wide by 7.6 cm high) would result in admission of enough vapor in most cases to create a glazed texture very similar to the one outside the container. Glaze patterns accumulate according to the shapes of holes cut in the walls of saggers, so that a series of these containers may suggest suitable forms to be placed within them; or the process could be reversed and saggers made to fit a group of objects.

Combustible materials placed within the saggers can leave fire prints on the pieces as they release organic compounds in gaseous form. Straw, seaweed, fruit, nuts, leather, sawdust, leaves, twine, and paper are only a few of the organic materials that can be used in this manner. The space between the wall of the sagger and the object can be stuffed with the organic matter prior to stacking. Careful note taking ought to accompany such trials, and pieces may be fired several times to reveal various possible effects.

The insides of the saggers can be painted with kiln wash or left to become glazed. Old saggers which have accumulated much vapor glaze may eventually give off enough volatile sodium to produce a delicate coat of glaze on objects fired within them, and the interiors could also be coated with glazes which mature at the anticipated firing temperature and may release volatile substances. Fritted and colemanite-based glazes might be used this way.

Other volatile agents designed to blush pieces in saggers can be painted on the interior walls—soda ash, for one, can be used alone or in combination with the metallic oxides and carbonates, as can sulfates and chlorides.

Slips and colorants can, of course, be sprayed onto the piece through the holes in the sagger to create patterns in stencil fashion.

One of the characteristics of sagger-fired wares is that they exhibit gradations of glaze accumulation in more or less controlled patterns. A great deal can be learned about the color potential of clays by firing them in this manner, since sodium vapor firing tends to extend the palette one might have come to accept with more conventional firing techniques.

Gravity and Glaze Flow. As glazes melt, some have a tendency to gather and flow, and ceramists have capitalized on this effect as well as having been victimized by it. Flow lines, however, can usually be anticipated as following straight down the side of an object from "top" to "bottom." Special setting arrangements, however, can vary this pattern and produce some desirable effects. Thrown or handbuilt forms can be made to support an object in a position different from the one it will occupy after the firing, causing the flow of glaze to travel in an unanticipated pattern. Ash glazes, with their characteristic flow lines, lend themselves to such treatment in the salt kiln, as do slips which have a tendency to streak and run.

Conclusion

Stacking a kiln for a vapor-glaze firing is a tedious and finicky task. It invariably takes longer than imagined and often creates an atmosphere of resignation among the participants—especially if the kiln is large—90 cu. ft (2.7 cu m) or larger. There are reminders everywhere that the medium will eventually render shelves and supports useless, and the placing of many small objects on their wads may drain one's nervous energy like no other phase of ceramics. Lighting the burners after the door is in place is often accompanied by a sense of relief. One's powers of conviction about the process are usually restored as flames warm the chamber and the firing cycle begins.

CHAPTER SEVEN

SOURCES OF SODIUM AS A VAPOR GLAZE

Salt, by virtue of its wide distribution and relative cheapness, is the traditional source of sodium in vapor glazing. Until comparatively recently it was the only feasible material available for such purposes. While alternatives to sodium chloride will be discussed later in the chapter, a brief look at the material itself may be of interest.

Common salt (NaCl) is often known as halite, or rock salt, to distinguish it from a class of chemical compounds known as "salts." It is essential to the health of humans and animals. Table salt is finely granulated, and, being hygroscopic (moisture-attracting), contains additives to keep it free-flowing. Small quantities of sodium aluminosilicate, tricalcium phosphate, or magnesium silicate are added for this purpose. Pure rock salt usually contains none of these additives.

Salt is used in the manufacture of sodium bicarbonate (baking soda), sodium hydroxide (caustic soda), hydrochloric acid, chlorine, and many other chemicals, as well as in the food-processing and meat-packing industries. It is widely used in cold climates to melt ice, and it is employed in water softeners to remove magnesium and calcium compounds.

The Greeks and Romans often used salt as an offering in religious rituals, where its characteristics as a preservative led to its symbolic representation of enduring qualities. Arabs use the expression, "There is salt [fidelity] between us," and, in English, an individual is respected for being the "salt of the earth." Cakes of salt have been used as money in Africa and as stipend in the Roman armies. The word "salary" derives from the Roman "salarium"—an allowance of money for salt.

Most salt comes from mining rock-salt deposits, such as those occurring along the United States Gulf Coast, by evaporating sea water—which contains salt in a ratio of 3.5 to every 100 parts—or by processing natural brines, which occur in Great Britain and the eastern United States.

Salt as a Source of Sodium Vapor

It should interest any ceramist to know that salt melts at 1472°F (800°C)—far lower than the temperature at which most salt glazing is accomplished—and can be used in vapor glazing at raku or earthenware temperatures. As long as the clay body is mature (see Chapter 2), glaze will form as a surface coating and will influence slips and glazes by fluxing them.

To observe the process described above during a salt firing, one should wear glasses designed to protect the eyes from ultraviolet rays. Toss a tablespoon or two of salt into the firebox of the kiln when the maturing point of the clay is being reached. Individual grains hitting the hot bricks will be seen to liquify instantaneously, forming a vapor which will follow the paths of convection and draft in the kiln. Small quantities of salt may be tossed or blown directly onto the objects being fired, if care is taken to avoid creating unnecessarily runny effects, which can adhere the piece to a shelf or the floor of the kiln.

In passing from a solid to a gas, salt liquifies. In this state it is highly corrosive to refractories, especially those containing silica, which it attacks, causing spalling. Small amounts of salt introduced rather frequently—at 10 to 20 minute intervals—will cut down on refractory wear. By comparison, larger quantities of salt thrown in at one time may be less effective, since the charges volatilize more slowly, producing greater quantities of liquid salt. In older kilns, especially, large salt charges may cause a molten flow to leak from the kiln, which will solidify on contact with air. From 1 to 2 C (¼ to ½ l) of salt per charge may be considered average. Much more than this may choke off the rate of heat increase by lowering the temperature of the fireboxes.

Granulated salt, being of a fine texture, vaporizes readily as it enters the kiln, in some cases being sprinkled directly on the ware, as in groundhog kilns (see Chapter 5). The fine crystals are well suited to being blown into the chamber through a pipe attached to a vacuum cleaner motor, as well. Dendritic salt is the finest type manufactured, volatilizes extremely rapidly, and may be ordered through firms purchasing salt in large quantities.

Rock salt has a tendency to snap and pop when introduced into a hot kiln, at times creating dangerous projectiles, which may fly from the firebox with some force as far as 6 ft (1.8 m). For this reason, the use of goggles during saltings is urged, especially when using rock salt. The larger crystals present more surface area to the hot atmosphere, and, containing more moisture than smaller granules, disperse with greater force.

Block salt, used to feed livestock, can be used if broken into manageable chunks for insertion into the kiln; but large pieces, especially if damp, could explode from the release of steam within a chunk, possibly endangering the wares, bagwalls, and individuals nearby.

Jar, 1842. Probably fired in groundhog kiln, due to salt and / or ash deposit on side. American. The Brooklyn Museum.

(Below) Teapot by Rick St. John, Kansas.

(Bottom) Teapot by David Shaner, Montana. 10'' x 8'' (25.4 x 20.3 cm). 1970. Slip trailed with ash glaze, salt fired to cone 10.

Teapot by Ian Gregory, England. 1976.
Photo: Robin Lord.

(Above) Teapot by Curt Hoard, Minnesota. 18'' x 16'' (45.7 x 40.6 cm). 1976. Stoneware thrown body with slip-cast dolphin spout. Coil-formed handle; heavy engobe decoration when pot was wet. Fired to cone 10; 35 to 40 lb of salt used in 100 cu ft kiln. Photo: Linda Passon.

(Left) Teapot. About 1750. Staffordshire. White stoneware. Staffordshire potters were among the first to exploit the unusual brilliance and whiteness which occurs from salt glazing iron-free bodies. Victoria and Albert Museum.

(Right) Casserole by Robert Winokur, Pennsylvania. 10½'' x 14'' (26.7 x 35.6 cm). 1976. Stoneware with blue wood ash glaze, slips, and engobes. Fumed.

(Below right) Casserole by Les Miley, Indiana. 9'' x 11'' (22.9 x 27.9 cm). 1975. Stoneware with porcelain slip, flashed with cobalt, fired to cone 10.

(Below) Handbuilt bowl by Bill Clark, Pennsylvania. 15½'' x 16'' (39 x 40 cm). 1976. Iron diffusing into the glaze has created subtle variegated textures under a smooth surface.

(Bottom) Covered jar by Byron Temple, New Jersey. 9'' x 9'' (22.9 x 22.9 cm). Wet-combed. Photo: John Pfahl.

State of the Salt upon Introduction. The question of whether to use dry, damp, or wet salt seems to provoke much discussion. Those who favor dry salt point to the ease of handling the material, the lack of corrosive liquids near metal burners and gas pipes, and the simplicity of eliminating yet another step to the process. The damp salt proponents point to the notion that more vapors in the kiln assist in the dispersion of sodium, itself in vapor form, promoting better results. This variable is simply one more that must be explored and tested individually to determine its applicability. Wet salt certainly increases pollution from the kiln.

Before leaving the matter entirely, however, it can be said for certain that the introduction of water into any heat-containing structure is potentially dangerous. Water can volatilize, forming steam with explosive force, damaging a kiln, and creating an extremely dangerous situation for all concerned. If salt is to be dampened, it is best contained in paper packets when introduced into the kiln (see Methods of Introduction in this chapter).

Trace Minerals in the Salt. The presence or absence of trace minerals in any form of salt used in glazing is largely a matter of personal preference. The purity of the material is generally sought after, even though trace minerals such as magnesium and calcium do occur and are bound to have slight but noticeable effects on the quality of the glaze. They may either flux or inhibit the melting of the sodium-alumina-silicate glaze, depending on their concentration in the salt and the degree to which they are already present in the clay. So many types of clay are in use, and so many varieties of salt available, that experimentation can be conducted quite easily. While personal preferences for one kind of salt or another may develop, the differences among them will probably not be radical.

Drawbacks of Using Salt. The chief drawback to using salt is the liberation of chlorine gas, which accompanies the breakdown of sodium chloride at high temperatures. Water vapor, in the form of highly visible fog, is another drawback, especially where it may be mistaken for smoke from an uncontrolled fire (see Chapter 9, Special Considerations, Salt Kilns as Sources of Pollution).

Sodium Compounds Other than Salt

Several sodium-bearing compounds other than salt are: sodium bicarbonate ($NaHCO_3$), sal soda (Na_2CO_3),

Teapot by Kaete Brittin Shaw, New York. 15'' (38.1 cm). 1976. Oxide-stained porcelain clays, low-fire luster overglaze and decals. Photo: Robert Hanson.

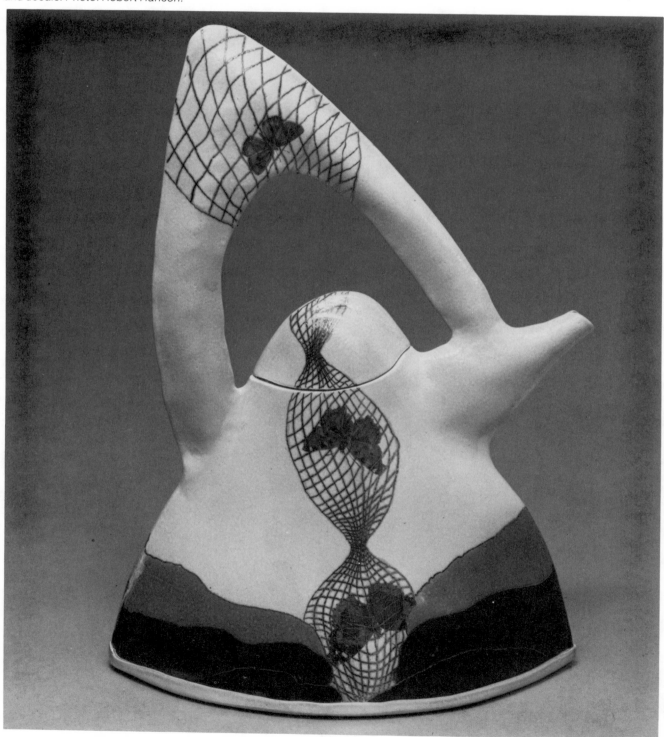

known also as sodium carbonate, washing soda, or soda ash, and monosodium glutamate ($NaOOCH_2 \cdot CHCH\ NH$) COOH), used in the food industry. At the present writing all have been used with varying degrees of success, either as substitutes for salt or in combination with it. Of the many sodium compounds these are among the cheapest and most available.

Sodium bicarbonate is perhaps the least expensive and most readily available salt substitute. It can be purchased in bulk (see Materials Suppliers at end of book) and is commonly referred to as baking soda.

The tendency of sodium bicarbonate to dissipate slowly in comparison to salt has been a problem, but the process can be hastened by spraying or blowing it into the kiln (see Methods of Introduction in this chapter). The glaze produced with sodium bicarbonate, while not identical to that made from salt, can be handsome, though the surface tends to be somewhat more "dry." The addition of 3%–10% borax to the baking soda may brighten the surface considerably, and if wood is used as a primary or secondary fuel (see Chapter 8, Salt-Firing Schedule), effects virtually indistinguishable from those obtained from salt vapors may be obtained.

The attractiveness of sodium bicarbonate as a salt substitute in glazing stems from the elimination of chlorine gas as a by-product in the process. With sodium bicarbonate, carbon dioxide, a relatively harmless gas, is produced, along with some water vapor.

Salt and sodium bicarbonate may be combined, which helps cut back on the less desirable effects of each. Sodium carbonate (soda ash) may also be combined with sodium bicarbonate, since in combination they disperse well, especially if blown into the kiln.

Experiments with various sodium compounds should be conducted in new kilns where salt has not been used, or at least new bricks should be installed in the firebox-bagwall areas, which retain the most residual sodium from previous salt firings. Residual sodium from salt may cause corrosive build-ups when sodium carbonate or soda bicarbonate are used. Generally speaking, similar amounts of these compounds could be used, but smaller quantities may be efficient if the damper is shut for a few minutes after the introduction of the material.

In using any salt substitute, the tendency is to want to reproduce the effects of "salt glazing," at the risk of by-passing visual and tactile qualities which might be best exploited for their own unique characteristics. One of

(Below) Plate by Lynn Maddox, California. 22'' x 6'' (55.9 x 15.2 cm). 1976. Stoneware.

(Bottom) Relief-molded dish (one of a pair). Staffordshire. About 1760. Stoneware. Victoria and Albert Museum.

the most inhibiting factors in the glazing of any type of ceramics is preconceiving desired effects. Comparatively few individuals seem willing to try such materials as sodium bicarbonate and soda ash because the surfaces are different from those they had anticipated, whereas the effects might well be used to esthetic benefit. This is an area where much more experimentation is needed and may be demanded as air-quality standards become more stringent.

Amounts of Sodium Compound

Several factors influence this decision, and can be posed as questions:

What Type of Surface Is Desired? Assuming the kiln is fired to a temperature sufficient to mature the body, glaze accumulation will be directly proportional to the amount of glazing material introduced. In a small kiln—30 cu ft (.9 cu m)—coated with alumina, or composed of high-alumina bricks, as little as 1 to 3 lb (.5 to 1.5 kg) of salt may be necessary to produce well-glazed objects. However, the same kiln made of unprotected brick may require much more salt, especially for first firings, since a comparatively small proportion of vapors ends up on the objects intended to be glazed.

What Type of Clay Will Be Used? Some clays, as mentioned in Chapter 2, are much more receptive to vapor glaze than others and require less sodium agent to be added to the kiln. However, a typical high-alumina clay with little free silica may take as much as three to four times the amount of agent to produce the same effect. The temperature at which glazing takes place is a further variable. Some clays may require much more sodium to produce a glaze at, say, cone 7–8, than they do at cone 10, when the silica may combine more readily with a smaller amount of vaporous sodium. Naturally, clay body experimentation will help determine this factor.

What Firing Methods Will Be Employed? Many variations in firing are practiced among contemporary ceramists. Some work with extremely tight kilns, using close damper control, and, in effect, are conservative in the way they retain sodium vapors in the kiln. Others use comparatively large amounts of glazing agents and give little heed to the obvious escape of great quantities of potential glaze-producing vapors. To a large degree, much of the ''bad press'' about salt glazing is due to such individuals. Simply stated, glazing operations fre-

Vase. 8" (20.3 cm). Thrown with elaborate applied floral decoration. Photographed in an old family tomb in Paris. Photo: Jack Troy.

Pipe. About 4'' (10 cm). German. Stoneware with silver lid, cherry-wood, ivory, antler, and horn stem. Keramion Gallery for Ceramic Art, Frechen.

(Below) Fleur de Job by Nancy Weeks Dudchenko, Pennsylvania. 36'' x 36'' (91.4 x 91.4 cm). 1976. Slab-built wall piece, high-fire stoneware clay and glazes to cone 10.

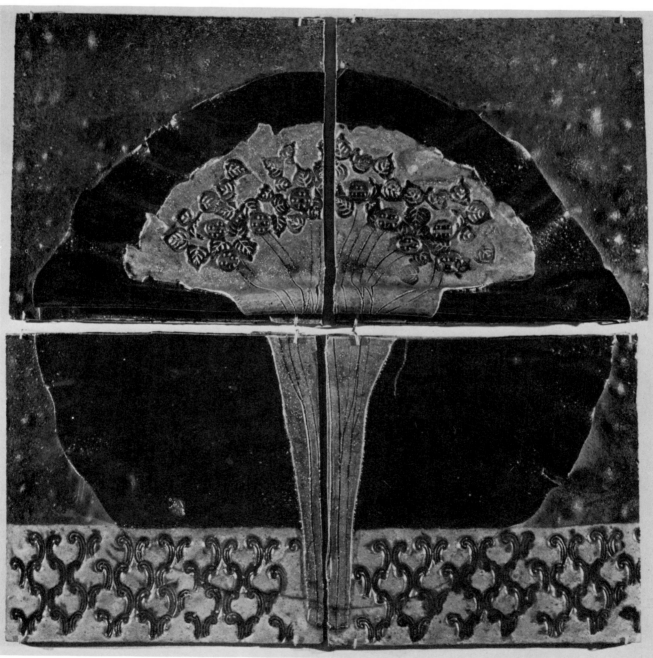

quently do not have to be as obvious as they often appear.

How Can Glaze Accumulation Be Measured? The best way during a firing is to use from 3 to 5 draw trials—rings of clay which are removed in sequence after specific amounts of glazing agent have been introduced. Since the draw trials are removed and cooled readily (they may be dunked in water immediately), they are invariably poor indicators of clay color but do show quite accurately the depth of glaze build-up.

What Is an Average Amount of Glaze Agent to Consider Introducing? About 10 to 20 oz (300 to 600 ml) per cu ft (.03 cu m) of kiln space.

Methods of Introduction

As with the decision of how much sodium compound to use, this is an area open to a wide range of possibilities.

(1) The simplest method is to toss the glazing agent into the firebox area through the port made for the same purpose (although the traditional German and groundhog kilns are salted through ports in the roof of the kiln, directly onto the wares). The compound can be loose, in which case it may scatter around outside the kiln with corrosive effects on most metals, or it may be made up into packets of newspaper or paper cups to be thrown or dropped into the firebox area. Plastic bags should *never* be used since they liberate extremely dangerous hydrocarbons when they burn.

(2) A simple metal pipe and plunger arrangement can be made by fitting a wooden handle onto a plug which slides piston-fashion in the pipe, pushing a charge of glazing agent out the end and into the firebox. A piece of angle iron about 3 by 3'' (7.6 by 7.6 cm) also works well, inserted in the port and tipped to one side to spill the charge into the firebox.

(3) The material can be blown into the kiln through a pipe inserted into the ports and connected to a compressed-air source or a vacuum-cleaner type of blower.

(4) Sodium brine solution may be dripped into the kiln if care is taken to regulate the flow evenly. Too much water vapor entering the kiln has explosive potential and must be guarded against. A gentle dripping of brine may be an effective means of producing a foggy vapor in the kiln, but would mean devising a noncorrosive holding

Metaphor *by Jack Troy, Pennsylvania. 12'' (30.5 cm). Stoneware with slips and glazes. Photo: Alex McBride.*

Sculptured jug by Cornwall E. Kirkpatrick at the Anna Potteries, Illinois. 12¼'' high, 11½'' in diam. (31 and 29.1 cm). Shows William "Boss" Tweed and his followers trying to climb into the money pot. Given to Thomas Nast in recognition of his powers as a caricaturist. Courtesy of The New-York Historical Society, New York City. Gift of Mrs. Thomas Nast.

container and flow regulator, along with a feeding pipe or tube directed into a firebox or other area. I personally would never use such a system due to the complications and potential safety hazard.

(5) Brine-soaked wood thrown into the kiln is yet another means of introducing the glazing agent. Salt and other compounds can be dissolved in a crock or bucket of hot water, stirring the liquid until saturated. Sticks of dry wood or wood shavings can then be soaked and introduced after they are dried (wet wood ignites slowly and may cause the kiln to lose heat). Dry wood ignites rapidly, dispersing sodium vapors along flame paths, often flashing objects to advantage. Long slivers and sticks of such wood may be painted with soluble colorants and pushed into the kiln to flash nearby pieces when they ignite. Porcelain clay is especially receptive to such random effects. A few sticks of wood about 1 by 1 by 12'' (2.5 by 2.5 by 30.5 cm), stoked sparingly during the salting, should show their effects on the ware.

The glaze produced in this manner may exhibit characteristics normally attributed to fortuitous "accidents" in firing and warrants exploration. Seaweed, salt-saturated sawdust, and most soft, porous woods will be found to work best. Such combustible agents can be made up some time in advance of the firing and dried to be used as needed. While large amounts of such supplementary fuel might be needed to add all the sodium in this manner, it should be tried by anyone willing to depart from a regular firing schedule, since it is an alternative with considerable potential for certain effects unobtainable by other means.

(6) Another method, long in use in central France, is that of placing salt in small—¼ to ½ c (.025 to .05 l)—clay containers throughout the kiln among the ware. As the temperature increases, sodium vapors permeate the kiln, flashing the pieces. Pottery made in the vicinity of LaBorne, near Henrichemont, south of Bourges, is an example of the effectiveness of this technique. Here the kiln reaches approximately cone 12; the ware is vitreous, and sodium vapors do not produce an orange-peel effect, but show up as subtle highlights, often with pleasing shifts in clay tonality. No additional salt is thrown into the kiln during the firing.

(7) An experimental technique in recent use consists of placing one or more objects to be vapor glazed in a sagger, together with a cup containing salt and/or various combinations of borax, sodium carbonate, and sodium bicarbonate. As the soda compound volatilizes, the objects in the container become glazed, and, since they are in a confined space, very little glazing agent is required. The inside of the sagger may be coated with alumina hydrate or other sodium-resistant wash if desired. Small cups may be thrown, bisqued, and used to hold 1 or 2 tablespoons of say, 90% salt and 10% borax, or 50% sodium carbonate and 50% sodium bicarbonate. Pots in such saggers should be placed on wads in case the glaze-producing material flows out of the cup. Although this method needs more investigation, it remains a tantalizing alternative to conventional salt glazing because of the possibility of producing sodium-glazed objects without the need for a special kiln. Since vapors would be contained in the sagger, virtually no atmospheric effluents would come from the process. Several promising trials along these lines were done at the NCECA Conference at Louisiana State University and at the Penland School of Crafts in the summer of 1976. A surprisingly small amount of vapor agent was sufficient to produce obvious results, although some substances such as borax, which assists vaporization, left undesirable residual deposits in the saggers.

CHAPTER EIGHT
SALT-FIRING SCHEDULE

In this chapter the procedure for firing a salt kiln will be discussed. Although the firing schedule that works best in a given kiln for particular results may vary, general guidelines are provided here for getting acquainted with the method.

Time Required for Salting

The presence of intense heat can be considered a catalyst for bringing about the interplay between sodium, silica, and alumina, which together produce a salt glaze. The usual temperature at which salt is introduced into the kiln is between cone 4 and cone 10 (although vapor glazing, as mentioned earlier, may be conducted at lower temperatures through the addition of fluxes to the body and perhaps to the vapor-producing agent). When cones consistent with the maturing temperature of the clay are falling inside the kiln the salt breaks down readily, since the fireboxes—where sodium compounds are normally introduced—are considerably hotter than the cones placed among the ware would indicate. Also, silica molecules in the clay body are particularly receptive to union with those of sodium, especially if the body contains "free" or chemically uncombined silica (see Chapter 2, Information on Clay Bodies).

The length of time during which salting takes place in a firing cycle can vary widely. Some potters wish to get the process over with and will salt in rather large amounts comparatively few times, while others may extend this aspect of firing for several hours. Since the introduction of salt frequently has a stalling effect on heat rise, the length of time during the melting of the cones may be prolonged considerably when compared to a typical oxidation or reduction firing. From 1 to 3 hours between cone 8 and cone 10 is not an uncommonly long period during which to introduce the salt.

There appear to be several advantages to salting over a fairly long period of time: (1) Excess molten salt which may flow out of the kiln, creating both the danger of fire and a personal safety hazard, will be avoided. (2) Glazing seems to be somewhat more even throughout the kiln. (3) Smaller amounts of salt introduced over a period of several hours provide more control over the atmosphere within the kiln, since oxygen is consumed as salt is broken down; the greater the quantity of salt introduced, the more the kiln may tend to reduce. (4) Colors and textures of slips and glazes are often enhanced by exposure to the vaporous atmosphere for longer periods. The development of "hare's-fur" streaks and warm tones in the clay and slips are more apt to occur than in fast firings. (5) With heavy salting, the accumulation of large quantities of liquid, molten salt in the fireboxes may hasten spalling of the refractories. (6) The danger of large quantities of hot chlorine gas being liberated in the vicinity of the kiln is lessened (see Chapter 9 on Toxicity).

Salt-firing Process

No written instructions can substitute for experience or the willingness to experiment during the salting itself and to note carefully the variations from one firing to the next.

Damper control. Manipulation of the damper during salting is a means of controlling the atmosphere and rate of heat gain in the kiln. Much of the vaporous sodium is driven up the chimney with ineffectual results to the ware, so that closing the damper will help retain the atmospheric conditions in the kiln most conducive to the development of well-glazed ware. A careful watch must be maintained, however, so as not to choke off temperature gain, overreduce the ware, or lose temperature.

Typical Salting. A typical salting might proceed as follows: when cone 8 is flat and cone 9 is softening, each burner pot is charged with 2c (½ l) of salt (this can be done with the aid of a scoop to better spread the salt within the kiln), and the damper is pushed in for 5 to 10 minutes while the vapors remain in the kiln. The damper is then opened to its normal position when the salt has disappeared from the fireboxes and the atmosphere in the kiln has cleared somewhat. The process is then repeated as many times as necessary, and eventually a rhythmical correlation is found between a given amount of salt and the period of time judged to be most effective for its introduction.

Temperature Rise. Individual kilns vary widely in the degree to which temperatures rise and fall during periods of salting and damper manipulations, but generally, from cone 8 upwards, abrupt temperature changes are rare, particularly since the hard-surface bricks or castables necessitated by the process retain heat very evenly, as a rule. One generally seeks a gradual rise in temperature during salting with 30 minutes to 1 hour or more elapsing between cones.

*Earth Band V by Les Miley, Indiana. 17''
high (43.2 cm). 1975. Stoneware jar,
slipped, sprigged, and incised.
Fired to cone 10.*

(Below) Form by Betty Woodman, Colorado. Porcelain glazed
with residual soda.

(Bottom) Footed bowl by Lynn Maddox, California. 12'' x 6''
(30.5 x 15.2 cm). 1976. Pulled handles.

Health Hazards. The hazard to health during this phase of the firing is greatest, and utmost caution should be observed to avoid contacting the fumes which may be liberated around the kiln, particularly if the damper is partially closed. Some of these vapors are readily seen under strong light, but such is not always available, nor should it be assumed that only visible fumes are dangerous (carbon monoxide, a potentially lethal gas, is invisible). Hot vaporous hydrochloric acid is injurious to sensitive tissues in the respiratory tract, the mucous membranes, and the eyes. Protective masks of the type mentioned in Chapter 9 on Safety Considerations should always be used during salting in enclosed places. To neglect this factor is to endanger oneself and incur possible permanent injury.

Kiln Deterioration. Older kilns have a tendency to develop cracks in the walls, under the arch, and around the door. While small cracks may not appear to be serious defects, they should be sealed with clay or refractory mortar to prevent vapor seepage during firing. The addition of a 4½" (11.4 cm) layer of insulating brick backing up the hot face can be staggered in courses so as to overlap the mortar joints of the inner course, and, further, a layer of mineral-wool block insulation, ceramic fiber insulation, and/or transite will help to insure a tight kiln. Arches can be covered with blanket mineral-wool insulation, some of which is available with wire-mesh backing, permitting it to be draped over curved surfaces. However, since the material is not weatherproof and disintegrates rapidly when wetted, it must be roofed over or covered directly with rolled sheet aluminum roofing.

Atmospheric Variables during Firing

Historically, most salt-glazed wares were fired in oxidizing atmospheres. Since the clays used were, by preference, of a low-iron content, the bodies burned to cream, buff, or light-gray tones, as in the case of Bennington ware. Most English vapor-glazed wares were white. Many of the pieces produced by the Cowden and Wilcox pottery in Harrisburg, Pennsylvania, apparently containing small amounts of iron in some form, were fired under partially reducing conditions and were often ochre or tan-orange in color. The potters of western Pennsylvania often produced very dark gray pots, the cobalt decoration frequently showing up as black or muddy brown in contrast with the bright blue of Bennington ware. This indicates that these particular kilns may have been less responsive to atmospheric changes, that the clays contained considerable iron, or that the formulas for decorating slips varied greatly. The salt-glazed wares of the Southern Piedmont area were wood fired, primarily in groundhog-type kilns. They are often distinctively gray-brown, or even green, due to the high-iron clays, which salt to dark celadon hues, the iron diffusing into the clear salt glaze. These regional variations in the character of wares are beneficial to today's studio potter, for they indicate how both obvious and subtle differences in surface textures and tones can be a direct result of the firing process and the nature of the materials, over which the contemporary ceramist has considerable control.

Oxidation and Reduction Atmospheres. Before discussing the aspects of oxidation and reduction firing as they apply to salt glazing, these terms should be reviewed by way of background. An oxidizing condition in a fuel-burning kiln is said to exist when air and gas are in such a proportion as to produce a flame, at which time the carbon in the fuel is combined with oxygen in the air to produce heat and carbon dioxide. An oxidizing atmosphere is considered stable as long as the fuel and oxygen are combined in the same ratio. If, however, a greater amount of fuel than air enters the kiln, some free carbon is liberated, as well as carbon monoxide, which is chemically active at high temperatures, and seeks to combine with oxygen in any form. This unstable atmospheric condition, known as reduction, produces markedly different visual effects in ware, since the activated carbon (in the form of carbon monoxide) extracts, or "reduces," oxygen molecules from the clay, glaze, bricks, or any reducible oxide with which it comes in contact.

A reducing atmosphere is usually created by cutting back on the air supply to the burner, or by pushing in the damper by degrees, which will produce a hazy atmosphere in the kiln along with lazy, rolling flames and, if reduction is heavy, sooty, cloudy smoke at the peepholes and chimney. (Heavy reduction wastes fuel, is a health hazard, and is unnecessary to obtain good results.)

During a conventional reduction firing, the reducing cycle may begin at around cone 08—the object being to reduce the clay body while the unmelted glaze is permeable. (Reduction which is postponed until glazes have begun to melt may result in pale, cement-colored clay and glazes which lack the depth and tonal variations associated with this type of firing.) This atmospheric condition may be maintained throughout the firing or modified as desired, but is usually maintained through the later stages of firing. It is, of course, the visual and tactile results of the chemical process described which account for the popularity of reduction-fired ceramics in recent years. Colors and textures are apt to be soft, warm, and aesthetically appealing, even though results from one firing to another may vary considerably. The results of a satisfactory reduction firing depend on several factors: (1) the quality of the reduction atmosphere, (2) the length of time to which ceramic materials are exposed to the atmosphere, and (3) the degree to which reducible oxides are present in clays, slips, glazes, or other raw materials.

The effects of oxidation firing in a salt kiln are certainly worthy of investigation and should not be thought of in the negative sense, as they often are when reduction is sought but not attained. Glazes reverting to their oxidized state during cooling can be particularly handsome, especially when deeper layers of the glaze retain reduction effects. Clay colors will be lighter in value, and the body itself may be stronger and more resistant to heat shock for not having been reduced (a necessary attribute for mugs, teapots, and casseroles). In addition, flame impingement may not discolor the ware or "flash" it, as is more likely to occur in reduction firing. Slips and glazes are apt to exhibit more intense hues in oxidation firings. Kilns which have both oxidizing and reducing areas in their stacking space are often found to produce wares of considerable beauty, since each atmospheric condition is conducive to effects which can be viewed appreciatively, as one's aesthetic values undergo change from firing to firing over a period of time.

Ceramists whose experience includes successful firings in fuel-burning kilns are at a distinct advantage when firing a salt kiln since the challenges implicit are similar to, but generally more involved than, those required for reduction firings.

To begin with, a whole range of body colors is possible in salt glazing, due to the interaction of the clay with the sodium-bearing vapors, which may take place under a variety of atmospheric conditions within the kiln. Any given clay may have a greater potential for developing tonal variations in salt glazing than if it were fired to the same temperature in either an oxidation or reduction atmosphere. This is due in part to the tendency of certain forms of iron to migrate to the surface of the clay

and become suspended in the vaporous glaze, diffusing through many color variations on a single object. The object's proximity to open flame has much to do with such possibilities, as does the composition of the body itself.

Firing Variations and Their Effects

The manipulation of the kiln atmosphere during firing, together with the great variety of clay body, glaze, and slip combinations, account for some of the creative possibilities during vapor-glaze firings. For example, clay bodies containing 1%–3% iron oxide and fired in a more or less continuously reducing atmosphere from, say, cone 08, may show only traces of vapor glazing, while the same body reduced at later stages of firing may pick up more glaze in which the iron becomes diffused in values of ochre, deep brown, or any of the celadon hues. The degree to which such phenomena occur seems to vary with the amount of flame impingement a piece receives, together with the factors governing reduction already mentioned.

Considering the clay surface variations which are created mainly by the placement of objects in the kiln, one can readily see how changes in any given atmospheric factor will influence the flow of combustion gases, often producing dramatic effects on the ware.

One such example is the combining of fuels during a firing. Propane, a fuel in common use, burns with a short, intensely hot flame, rather localized in nature. Adding wood strips or splinters to the fireboxes prior to and during the salting creates an entirely different quality in the kiln, characterized by long, penetrating flames which tend to disperse the sodium vapors evenly throughout the chamber—a factor of perhaps somewhat greater importance to the producer of smaller wares than to the sculptor. Wood-fired vapor-glazed objects may also tend to be brighter, exhibiting flashings, ash deposits, and other surface characteristics which distinguish them from wares fired with natural gas or fuel oil, each of which, of course, may have its advantages.

Draw Trials

During the vapor-glazing cycle of the firing, draw trials—small loops of clay—can be withdrawn through spyholes on a stout wire or iron rod to check the progressive build-up of glaze. Approximately five draw trials might be removed at various times during the salting and lined

Perfection Filter (water filter), 10″ high, rim 9″ diam. (25.4, 22.9 cm). 1875–82. N. A. White & Son. Molded salt-glazed stoneware with cobalt slip. Muson-Williams-Proctor Institute

(Below) Cup with figure and flower *by Tom Suomalainen, North Carolina. 6''* (15.2 cm). 1976. Fired to cone 6 with Albany slip liner. Flower is porcelain. Photo: Evon Streetman.

(Bottom) Horse and Rider *by Jeanne L. Stevens-Sollman, Pennsylvania. 27'' x 22'' x 12''* (68.6 x 55.9 x 30.5 cm). Stoneware and porcelain. Vapor glazed with 18 lbs of sodium bicarbonate in a 60 cu ft kiln, fired to cone 9.

up for comparison, after having been cooled in air or water. One's normal clay body should be used for these trials, and they may be considered a fairly accurate measure of glaze accumulation but will have little to do with the color of the pieces which come from the kiln after having cooled more slowly.

Effects of Rates of Cooling

As a rule of thumb, one should assume that cooler tones in clays, slips, and glazes result from rapid cooling, while slower post-firing heat losses will produce darker, warmer values, other factors being equal. Hard firebrick retains heat much longer than the soft, or insulating, brick often used in reduction kilns, and the cooling cycle may be somewhat longer than expected. After firing off, or reaching the desired temperature, one might shut off all the burners, seal the burner ports, shut the damper, or decide to maintain a steady, soaking heat for half an hour or more to smooth out slips or glazes which tend to pinhole from gases escaping from the clay. Sodium vapors linger in the kiln for perhaps several hours after the final salting, and a soaking period tends to promote the development of "hare's-fur" or "partridge-feather" streaks and some forms of titanium or zinc crystals which may develop in certain slips and glazes.

After an hour or so of more or less constant temperature, the damper could be opened slightly and the kiln allowed to cool of its own accord, assisted periodically by removing bricks from the outer door, if a loosely stacked door is used.

Another possibility is to cool the kiln as rapidly as is safely possible at the conclusion of the firing—a technique often used prior to fuming, a process discussed later in this chapter.

Fast cooling consists of opening all or several of the parts of the kiln which regulate the passage of air through the structure—burner ports, salting ports, spyholes, damper, and the door. At the conclusion of a firing, the upper ports could be opened, and the top courses of door brick removed (from as few as one course to as many as six or eight). Convection—the tendency of hot air to rise—will boost heat out of the kiln through the door if the damper is shut. If the damper is open, thereby drawing air through the door, most heat will be lost through the chimney, with some radiant heat being dissipated through the doorway. If the burner ports are opened in addition to the damper, cooling at

*Doorstop in form of poodle.
19th century American.
The Brooklyn Museum.*

the bottom of the kiln, which always occurs faster than at the top, will be hastened. Variations here are many, including closing the damper while opening the burner ports to cool through the door. Other combinations involve crossdrafts and convection.

Compared to "normal" firing procedures, the foregoing may seem like a radical departure, involving considerable risk to the ware and to individuals, but if the firing is conducted with care, the dangers can be minimized and the process engaged in quite safely.

Safety Considerations during Cooling. To begin with, crowded conditions around the kiln should be eliminated. One or two persons can take down the door bricks better than any other number of well-intentioned helpers, who should remain at some distance from the kiln. Hot bricks are potentially dangerous. They should be handled with raku tongs and heavy insulated gloves. Door bricks coated with alumina hydrate fuse to each other less rapidly and will separate quite easily (see Chapter 6 on Stacking); older bricks with some glaze build-up may have to be gently pried apart before removal. These bricks should be stacked neatly nearby as they come from the kiln, red-hot. They are susceptible to cracking and should not be dropped. Hot pieces of clay wadding used to chink up the door burn quickly through thin shoes and must be kept swept away. This is a good time to be fastidious and a dangerous one to be lackadaisical.

Fast-cooling Effects. The results of fast cooling will vary according to the clays, slips, and glazes used and the type of firing cycle employed. Generally, color values will be lightened and sharpened. The vapor glaze may tend to show greater light-refractory qualities, and some of the adverse effects of reduction, such as muddy tones in the body and slips, may be lessened.

Some adverse effects should be mentioned. The kiln, clay body, and shelves may undergo strain and can be weakened, unless one is careful not to prolong the fast cooling past dull red-heat and into the quartz-inversion stage, at 1063°F/573°C, when rapid cooling can cause considerable cracking (some of it audible) to any refractory material. As pieces within the kiln lose color, the door bricks should be replaced and the rate of cooling slowed by closing the damper and sealing the burner ports.

Fuming, a Post-firing Process

A method of imparting iridescence to the surface of fired ceramic objects has been adapted from a practice apparently discovered by glassblowers. Essentially, a rainbowlike effect, known to physicists as "thin film interference"—a visual phenomenon like that of gas or oil on water—is imparted to objects in a kiln by using residual heat from the firing to break down compounds that release metallic vapors, which settle on the glazed surfaces they contact. Stannous chloride is one of many substances commonly used in the process; others include ferric chloride, strontium nitrate, barium chloride, chromium nitrate, and bismuth nitrate.

Fuming should be done just as the red-heat of the firing has dissipated from the kiln—a condition best determined visually. Depending on weather conditions, the size of the kiln, the degree to which the kiln is insulated, and the position of the damper during cooling, the proper temperature to fume may occur within 2 to 8 hours after firing off. Generally the bottom of the kiln will cool first, and the metallic crystals may be thrown onto the hot bricks in the fireboxes or near the spyhole, where they will vaporize immediately. Opening the damper draws the fumes out the flue so that they will not permeate the upper portions of the kiln, which may be too hot to produce the desired effects. An hour or two later the upper portion of the kiln may be fumed and vented out through the spyholes near the top, while the damper is kept closed.

Fuming which takes place much above or below 1292°F/700°C will appear as foggy, semiopaque film, and the object may have to be refired to erase the unwanted characteristics. Also, fuming agents which contact the ware directly may produce disagreeable, scummy effects necessitating refiring.

Kiln Location for Fuming. A number of factors will enter into this aspect of the firing, one of which is the location of the kiln. Since the disappearance of dull red color in the kiln is the best indicator of the proper fuming temperature, a kiln located in an area which can be darkened will be somewhat more versatile than one entirely outdoors. For salt kilns that are outdoors, the firing cycle may have to be revised so that the area is dark when fuming is to be done.

Alternate Fuming Techniques. Methods of fuming may vary from the one described above. A "wand" can be

*Covered jar by John Glick, Michigan. 5''
x 5'' (12.7 x 12.7 cm). Porcelain with
soda ash vapor glaze. Cobalt oxide decoration with celadon and ash glazes.
Fired to cone 10.*

made by plugging one end of a piece of pipe into which has been drilled a number of holes near the plugged end. The pipe could be heated simply by sticking it into the kiln. The crystals slid down to the heated end would then vaporize out through the holes and onto the ware. By carefully manipulating the pipe within the kiln through several spyholes or ports, pieces can be selectively fumed, as desired, with the aid of a flashlight.

Another method consists of dissolving the fuming agent in alcohol or water and spraying it into the kiln, but the volatile, potentially explosive aspect of this technique makes it, in my mind, inadvisable.

Smaller pieces may be removed from the kiln with tongs and held over a heated can containing the fuming agent, then replaced in the kiln to cool.

Cooling the Kiln. After fuming, the kiln should be cooled rather slowly, as quartz inversion may crack those pieces which are subjected to drafts or rapid temperature change.

Safety Considerations. Utmost care should be used when handling materials used in fuming, as they may cause skin irritations. Inhaled vapors may be toxic. Wear rubber gloves and a safety respirator in addition to goggles when fuming. Maintain good ventilation at all times.

Results of Fuming. Fuming can lend a heightened appearance to an entire object, or to one part of a piece, creating subtle and mysterious iridescent highlights. As in the case of any decorative process, however, one must judge how to avoid overdoing the desired effect. Blatant, garish iridescence on an otherwise well-con-ceived object may cheapen its appearance and emphasize surface values to the point where they dominate the other considerations sought in an integrated piece of work.

Conclusion

The firing process in salt glazing might be considered a ritual in which there are countless variations—some appropriate and fortuitous, others to be avoided at all costs. The basis for such judgments must be discovered individually within the context of an ever-developing sense of acceptance or rejection of the objects which come from the kiln. These judgments grow out of one's continual exposure to the firing cycle: the regulated progression of heat, the attainment of a precisely determined temperature, and the period of cooling.

Work in any area of ceramics may undergo great changes as a result of the firing process, but, with salt glazing in particular, the possibility exists for a heightened sense of awareness of the dramatic qualities implicit in each firing. Salt sacrificed in the firebox will be torn apart into its irreducible chemical components and liberated as an unstable vapor. Some of the sodium will combine with other elements to establish new identities. On the creative level, these transformations are brought about by the desire of an individual to *participate* in a process, not necessarily to control it. The degree to which one feels comfortable or capable of acting imaginatively in such circumstances is a highly personal matter, and helps account for the significant difference in approach to be noted in surveying the work of contemporary ceramists working in this medium.

CHAPTER NINE

SPECIAL CONSIDERATIONS

It is difficult to discuss toxicity of materials and safety procedures without sounding like a scoutmaster. Participation in any aspect of ceramics demands awareness of the possible dangers involved in exposure to toxic materials. Working in a well-ventilated lab, wearing a dust mask when weighing out clay and glaze ingredients, and washing the hands thoroughly after handling hazardous materials are several precautions which should be habitual.

Preventive Techniques

Chapter 5, The Salt Kiln, stressed the importance of adequate ventilation in the vicinity of the kiln, particularly with reference to seepage of vapors through cracks in the door and between the bricks of older structures. These vapors can be toxic—particularly vaporous hydrochloric acid if salt is being used as the glazing agent, but small amounts of zinc, barium, chromium, cobalt, and other heavy metals may be present as well—and should not be inhaled. Carbon monoxide, a deadly, colorless gas produced during reduction cycles, is heavier than air and may accumulate along floors. Plenty of open doors and windows, rotating ventilators on kiln-house roofs, and large ventilating fans of the type found in dairy barns can be use to advantage in keeping air moving around a firing kiln if it is located indoors.

Possible eye damage may occur over a period of time unless adequate protection is taken while firing kilns. Vapor glazing usually calls for rather frequent inspection of conditions within the kiln, and, while the eyes may adjust to the intense glare of high temperatures, making the need for glasses seem unnecessary, the retinas of the eyes may in time undergo dangerous subjection to ultraviolet rays and be permanently damaged.

Ordinary sunglasses are not adequate protection. Glasses or goggles specifically designed for screening ultraviolet rays should be used (see Materials Suppliers in the Appendix). Such glasses should be owned and used by all ceramists and glassblowers.

Burns are a frequent occurrence to ceramists working around vapor-glaze kilns. Many can be prevented. Heavy leather, asbestos-lined gloves such as those worn by welders are good protection during a firing, and, although they may be expensive, will outlast the cheap asbestos gloves commonly in use in many studios. Treat any burn promptly and have first-aid supplies on hand.

Spyhole and burner-port bricks could have their hot ends coated with alumina hydrate to prevent confusion when they are withdrawn and set down. Removing hot door bricks is best done by one person. Leather shoes, long pants, and a long-sleeved shirt should be worn at all times when handling bricks, loading, and firing.

Some persons may exhibit sensitivity to certain compounds, especially those used in fuming. Stannous chloride should never touch bare skin. Although its effects are not extremely caustic, prompt and thorough washing after accidental contact is necessary. Extreme caution must be used to avoid breathing vaporous agents used in fuming and to keep the fumes from contacting the mucous membranes. Use rubber gloves when handling fuming agents.

Masks, specifically those designed for silica and fine particulate matter, should always be used when mixing clay and glaze (see Materials Suppliers in the Appendix).

Gas masks should be worn during the firings when vapor-producing agents are introduced if the kiln is in an enclosed area (see Materials Suppliers in the Appendix).

The hazards in vapor glazing are considerably greater than in more conventional procedures. Salt which melts and flows out of the fireboxes may be red-hot and ignite leaves near an outdoor kiln, melt substances used to prevent gas leaks at pipe connections, and cause burns. Hot rock salt may explode from the kiln with considerable force, endangering eyes and skin. Hot sodium vapors pushed from the kiln at spyholes may inflict burns, and one should stand well back while removing draw trials and checking cones.

The danger of cuts from sharp fragments on kiln shelves and kiln interiors has been mentioned in Chapter 5.

The Salt Kiln and Pollution

Salt kilns are well known as sources of pollution, both visual and chemical. In some areas they have been shut down and frequently are cited as being undesirable, particularly on college campuses and in areas of high population density.

Much of this criticism is well deserved. While many aspects of ceramics seem well adapted to populous areas, salt glazing, as it is presently practiced by the vast majority of ceramists, is not an activity to be welcomed by many persons lacking the zeal of the participants. Dense clouds of vapor and smoke accompanying the process are particularly offensive to anyone with a heightened

Jug, about 1850. American. Incised blue decoration. The Brooklyn Museum.

Slab platter by Curt Hoard, Minnesota.
18'' x 12'' x 6'' (45.7 x 30.5 x 15.2 cm).
1976. Stoneware drape-molded with
applied slip decoration. Fired to cone
10. Photo: Linda Passon.

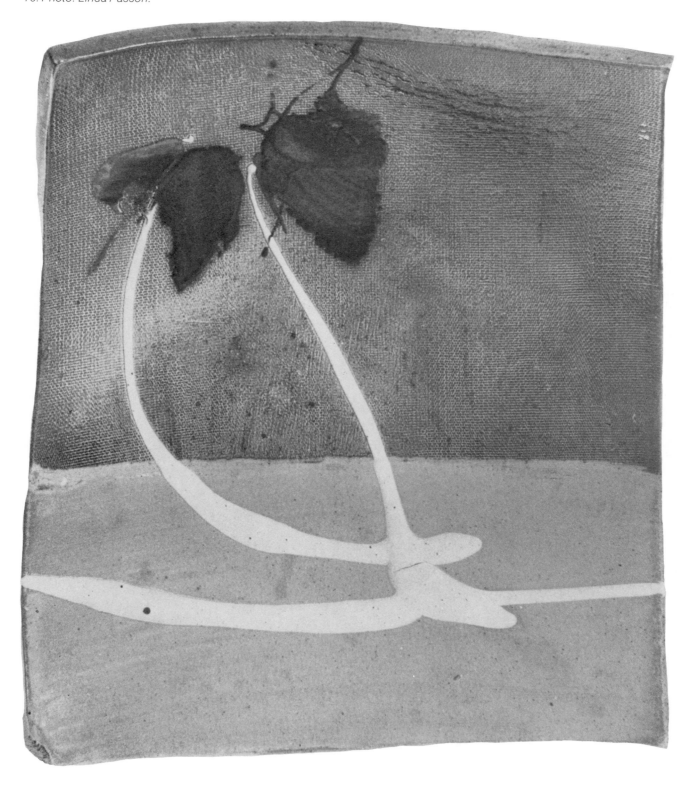

sense of consciousness about air quality. Although some potters may be able through care in firing procedures to alleviate many of the factors contributing to the visual pollution mentioned, often to the point where the process may be carried out fairly inconspicuously, others may simply have to practice this method of glazing in areas where kilns are relatively isolated. In an era of shrinking open spaces, this may seem to be a suggestion of limited usefulness; yet there is no reason to expect a neighbor to accept another's fog, even though its content may be relatively innocuous by the time it crosses the ceramist's property line. To anyone seriously concerned about air-quality standards, aesthetic motivation may come in a poor second when compared to the responsibility of each person to contribute to a collective effort to create and maintain a high-quality environment.

The dilemma is obvious. Some ceramists have abandoned the practice of salt glazing entirely, and one author of a ceramics text dismisses the subject with a single lofty sentence. The fact remains that most persons, even those who claim to function on a consistently creative level, slip easily into habitual patterns of behavior and become less concerned with the potential of alternatives than with doing what is most comfortable. Experimentation must sometimes take a back seat to the production of salable objects, but every kiln fired should contain some ''hunch''—some new clay body test, slip, colorant, glaze combination, or alternative firing procedure. It is easy to avoid the unfamiliar, and this tendency in salt glazing may seal the fate of the practice, if it precludes objective investigation on the part of concerned individuals to seek alternative means of vapor glazing.

I can make a few personal suggestions along these lines, but solutions to the problem of environmental pollution must be met individually if we are to assume responsibility for the quality of our environment.

(1) Construct a small test kiln, insulate it well, and fire it frequently, using a variety of methods, clay bodies, and vapor agents. Try to dislodge preconceived notions of how vapor-glazed objects are ''supposed'' to look. Set aside some time each year to attend a workshop or meet with others who are concerned with examining alternatives to traditional methods of working if those methods are ''dirty.''

(2) Try, whenever possible, to fire on clear, windy days, when the barometer is rising. Vapors dissipate much more readily under such conditions.

(3) Avoid firing a salt kiln on a rainy, damp, overcast day. Vapors do not dissipate rapidly under such conditions, and in areas of high population density the accumulation of thick clouds is certain to create hostility among some observers. If firings under these conditions seem unavoidable, one must be prepared to justify the acitivty in the face of genuine concern among those sharing the same environment. Arrogance or lack of cooperation on the part of the ceramist may result in the enactment of local ordinances and legislation which may penalize all persons with kilns.

(4) Closing the damper after introducing the vapor agent will almost certainly help reduce airborne pollution, as will reducing gas pressure somewhat during this cycle of the firing. If wood is used as the primary or supplementary fuel, stoking should be regular and light to avoid heavily reducing conditions and smoky exhaust at the chimney.

(5) One's work should undergo rigorous critical scrutiny to determine whether the objects truly demand a vapor-glazed surface, and, if they do, the degree to which glaze accumulation is necessary. Many objects appear to be overglazed, as if the person firing the kiln were not certain enough glaze was being produced. Ideally, those engaged in vapor glazing do so out of some sense of conviction that their work demands such a surface.

NOTES

Chapter One

1. John C. L. Sparkes and Walter Gandy. *Potters, Their Arts and Crafts* (London: S. W. Partridge & Co., 1896).

2. Simeon Shaw. *History of the Staffordshire Potteries* (New York: Praeger, 1970). Originally published by the author at Hanlet, England in 1829.

3. Llewellynn Jewett. *The Ceramic Art of Great Britain from Pre-Historic Times down to the Present Day* (London: Vitrue and Company, Ltd., 1878).

4. Lura Woodside Watkins. *Early New England Potters and Their Wares* (Sturbridge, Mass.: Old Sturbridge Village 1959), p. 38.

5. Harold Guilland. *Early American Folk Pottery* (Philadelphia: Chilton, 1971), p. 59.

6. Dorothy Auman. Seagrove Pottery, Seagrove, North Carolina. Conversation with author, March 1976.

7. Elmer Smith. *Pottery, A Utilitarian Folk Craft* (Lebanon, Pennsylvania: Applied Arts Publishers, 1972), p. 27.

8. Dr. Georgeanna Greer of San Antonio, Texas, is presently researching the origin and evolution of the groundhog kiln.

9. Janet R. MacFarland. "Nathan Clark, Potter," *Antiques* LX (July 1951), p. 42. Reprinted by courtesy of *The Magazine ANTIQUES.*

10. E. Atlee Barber. *Salt Glazed Stoneware: Germany, Flanders, England* (Philadelphia: The Pennsylvania Museum, 1901).

11. Sandra Johnstone, California potter, in letter to author.

Chapter Two

1. Donald Webster. *Early Canadian Pottery* (Greenwich, Connecticut: New York Graphic Society Ltd., 1971), pp. 121–122.

2. W. G. Lawrence. *Ceramic Science for the Potter* (Philadelphia: Chilton, 1972), p. 162.

3. L. E. Barringer. "The Relation between the Constitution of a Clay and Its Ability to Take a Good Salt Glaze," *Trans. Am. Ceramic Society* 4, pp. 211–229 (1902).

4. Robert L. Hess. Alumina-Silica Refractories Technician, North American Refractories Company, letter to author, June 13, 1975.

5. I don't know why and I wish I did. In the5 meantime, I have learned to live with the results.

6. Michael Cardew. Speech. NCECA Conference, Gatlinburg, Tennessee, March 1973.

7. Shoji Hamada. "Shoji Hamada," *Crafts*, September–October, 1975.

8. Susan Peterson. *Shoji Hamada* (Tokyo, New York, and San Francisco: Kodansha International, Ltd., 1975), p. 38.

Chapter Three

1. John C. L. Sparks and Walter Gandy. *Potters: Their Arts and Crafts* (London: S. W. Partridge and Company, 1896), p. 38.

2. Cullen W. Parmalee. *Ceramic Glazes* (Chicago: Industrial Publications, Inc., 1951), p. 180.

3. W. G. Lawrence. *Ceramic Science for the Potter* (Philadelphia: Chilton, 1972), pp. 165–166.

4. Dr. L. C. Werner Lehnhauser. *Glasuren und ihre Farben* (Dusseldorf: Wilhelm Knapp Verlag).

5. Tom Turner. "Producing Copper Red Salt Glazes," *Ceramics Monthly*, February 1974.

Chapter Five

1. Basic texts on the subject of kiln building which should be read prior to construction are: Daniel Rhodes, *Kilns* (Philadelphia: Chilton, 1974), Frederick Olsen's *The Kiln Book* (La Puente, California: Keramos, 1975), and Frank Colson's *Kiln Building with Space-Age Materials* (New York: Van Nostrand Reinhold, 1975).

THE POLLUTION ASPECTS OF SALT GLAZE FIRING

by Charles Hendricks, Professor of Nuclear & Electrical Engineering, University of Illinois, Urbana and Don Pilcher, Assistant Professor of Art, University of Illinois, Urbana.
From *Salt Glaze Ceramics*, publication of the American Crafts Council, New York, 1972.
Reprinted with permission of The American Crafts Council, New York (currently available).

The current intense interest in pollution has prompted many potters using salt kilns to question this process as a means of production. In addition, many government agencies, especially in metropolitan areas, have investigated and closed down salt kilns. For these reasons we have undertaken an examination of the pollution aspects of salt glazing. Hopefully our findings will give the potter and other interested parties some facts and solutions to the problem.

The following is an explanation of salt firing and its by-products. Note that variables may occur depending on fuels, kilns, clays, and salts used. The pollution factors of salt firing are twofold—the fuel and the salt.

Fuel

Natural gas, bottle gas, oil and wood are individually capable of producing the required temperatures for salting. In most cases these temperatures are cone 8 to cone 11 but salting can be done at lower temperatures with vitreous non-talc bodies. Of these fuels, natural and bottle gas are most easily regulated to produce an oxidation or reduction atmosphere. The difference between these kiln atmospheres is the key to controlling the color of the glaze as well as the polluting effluents.

In an *oxidation* atmosphere the fuel is completely combusted and the free carbon, hydrocarbon, and carbon monoxide by-products are kept at a minimum. Consequently the ware has a lighter or cleaner appearance and the kiln effluents consist almost entirely of water vapor and carbon dioxide. (Low grade fuels containing excessive sulphur can mar this purity.)

Reduction atmospheres are based upon incomplete combustion. An excess of fuel produces carbon which alters the color of the iron in the clay and consequently the glaze. Deeper and richer browns are produced in this way. A large quantity of this unburned fuel is emitted in the form of free carbon, relatively stable hydro-carbons, and carbon monoxide. These emissions are identical to those produced by power companies burning coal (with the exception of inorganic fly-ash), jets burning kerosene, or cars and trucks burning gasoline.

Salt

While salts vary—some contain traces of magnesium, calcium, or iodine—they are basically sodium chloride (NaCl). Upon introduction into the fire at advanced temperatures when the clay body is vitrifying, the salt dissociates into sodium and chlorine. The sodium unites with the alumina and silica in the clay to produce a glaze—a sodium, alumina silicate. Fuel + air + salt + clay = carbon dioxide (CO_2) + water (H_2O) + nitrogen (N_2) + sodium hydroxide (NaOH) + hydrogen chloride (HCl) + heat + glaze.

Some sodium and chlorine vapors are exhausted into the atmosphere during firing. These gases leave the kiln as condensation nuclei which have an affinity for moisture and thus produce a very noticeable fog. This fog is composed of hydrochloric acid and water fog droplets $(HCl.H_2O)$ condensed on sodium salt nuclei. In concentrated amounts or closed areas the hydrochloric acid vapor is highly toxic. Humans and steel are the most seriously affected. (Our salt kilns have been operating for four years in close proximity to trees, grass, shrubs and flowers with no ill effects.)

This hydrochloric acid fog will usually dissipate within fifteen minutes of the initial salt introduction as the reactions terminate and as the components become diluted in the atmosphere and the condensing drops grow large enough to fall to the ground. This fact however, does not diminish neighborly concern over the fog.

Since the object of salt glazing is to deposit a sodium vapor within the kiln, we recommend using other sodium compounds in place of salt, thereby eliminating the objectionable chlorine gases. Such compounds as sodium bicarbonate $(NaHCO_3,$ baking soda) and sodium carbonate $(Na_2CO_3,$ washing soda-sal soda) will work. This fact was noted by Cullen Parmelee in his book *Ceramic Glazes* written in 1948. When purchased in commercial quantities, the cost of these other compounds is not prohibitive.

When using these other sodium compounds it is advisable to introduce them in small amounts over a longer period of time. In this way one can avoid a saturation of sodium oxide in the fire box and thus prevent severe deterioration of the refractories.

Summary

We would like to make some comparisons between kiln firing and other combustion sources common to our present way of life. Variations occur, of course, from kiln to kiln, car to car, and airplane to airplane.

A 30 cubic foot kiln fired to cone 9 and salted consumes: 30 lbs. natural gas, 570 lbs. air, 25 lbs. salt. The elemental constituents of these materials are approximately: 22.9 lbs. carbon, 7.1 lbs. hydrogen, 114.0 lbs. oxygen, 456.0 lbs. nitrogen, 10.0 lbs. sodium (90% of which is deposited on the ware, bricks, kiln shelves), 15.0 lbs. chlorine.

This 30 cubic foot kiln produces these effluents in the final two hours of firing: 60.0 lbs. water vapor, 84.0 lbs. carbon dioxide, 456.0 lbs. nitrogen, 1.0 lb. sodium compounds, 13.5 lbs. chlorine as hydrochloric acid and other chlorine compounds.

When using sodium carbonate (Na_2CO_3) for glazing the reaction for complete combustion is: fuel + air + washing soda (Na_2CO_3) + clay = nitrogen (N_2) + carbon dioxide (CO_2) + sodium hydroxide (NaOH) + water (H_2O) + glaze.

With the exception of the sodium and chlorine compounds, the firing of this kiln for two hours is comparable—in energy consumed and effluents produced—to a car running at 70 mph for one hour or a 707 aircraft at cruising speed for three seconds.

It is not our intention to whitewash salt firing as a pollution source but to place it in proper perspective to the overall environmental picture. In this relationship, kiln firing is not a considerable pollution source.

BIBLIOGRAPHY

Books

Barber, Edwin Atlee. *Salt-Glazed Stoneware—Germany, Flanders, England, and the United States.* Philadelphia: Pennsylvania Museum and School of Industrial Art, 1906.

Behrens, Richard. *Glaze Projects.* Columbus, Ohio: Professional Publications, 1972.

Berensohn, Paulus. *Finding One's Way with Clay.* New York: Simon and Schuster, 1972.

Black, Harding, and Greer, Georgeanna. *The Meyer Family: Master Potters of Texas.* San Antonio, Texas: Trinity University Press, 1971.

Ceramics Digest. Wichita, Kansas: Wichita State University Potters Guild, 1976.

Colson, Frank. *Building Kilns from Space-Age Materials.* New York: Van Nostrand Reinhold, 1976.

Cooper, Emmanuel. *A History of Pottery.* New York: St. Martin's Press, 1972.

Coyne, John, ed. *The Penland School of Crafts Book of Pottery.* Indianapolis and New York: Bobbs Merrill, 1975.

Crawford, Jean. *Jugtown Pottery.* Winston-Salem, North Carolina: John F. Blair, Publisher, 1964.

Guilland, Harold. *Early American Folk Pottery.* Philadelphia: Chilton, 1972.

Hamer, Frank. *The Potter's Dictionary of Materials and Techniques.* New York and London: Pitman, Watson-Guptill, 1975.

Honey, W.B. *European Ceramic Art from the Middle Ages to about 1815.* London: Faber and Faber, 1896.

James, Arthur. *The Potters and Potteries of Chester County, Pennsylvania.* West Chester, Pa.: Chester County Historical Society, 1944.

Jewett, Llewellynn. *The Ceramic Art of Great Britain from Prehistoric Times Down to the Present Day.* London: Virtue and Company, 1878.

Ketchum, William C. Jr. *Early Potters and Potteries of New York State.* New York: Funk and Wagnalls, 1970.

Lawrence, W.G. *Ceramic Science for the Potter.* Philadelphia: Chilton, 1972.

Noble, Joseph Veach. *The Technique of Attic Painted Pottery.* New York: Watson-Guptill, and London: Faber and Faber, 1965.

Olsen, Fred. *The Kiln Book.* Bassett, California: Keramos Books, 1973.

Osgood, Cornelius. *The Jug and Related Stoneware of Bennington.* Rutland, Vermont, and Tokyo, Japan: Charles E. Tuttle Co. 1971.

Parmalee, Cullen. *Ceramic Glazes.* Chicago: Industrial Publications, Inc. 1951.

Peterson, Susan. *Shoji Hamada, A Potter's Way and Work.* New York: Kodansha, 1974.

Ramsay, John. *American Potters and Pottery.* New York: Tudor Publishing Co., 1947.

Rice, Alvin H. and Stoudt, John Baer. *The Shenandoah Pottery.* Shenandoah, Virginia: Shenandoah Publishing Co., 1929.

Ritchie, Ralph. *Gas Kiln Firing.* Bassett, California: Keramos Books, 1975.

Rhodes, Daniel. *Clay and Glazes for the Potter.* rev. ed. Pxiladelphia: Chilton, and London: Pitman, 1973.

———. *Kilns.* Philadelphia: Chilton, 1974.

———. *Stoneware and Porcelain.* Philadelphia: Chilton, 1974.

Sanders, Herbert. *Glazes for Special Effects.* New York: Watson-Guptill, 1974.

Shafer, Thomas. *Pottery Decoration.* New York: Watson-Guptill, and London: Pitman, 1976.

Shaw, Simeon. *History of the Staffordshire Potteries.* New ed. New York: Praeger, (1829), 1970.

Shepard, Anna O. *Ceramics for the Archaeologist.* Washington, D.C.: Carnegie Institute of Washington, 1971.

Smith, Elmer. *Pottery, A Utilitarian Folk Craft.* Lebanon, Pennsylvania: Applied Arts Publishers, 1972.

Soldner, Paul. *Kiln Construction.* New York: American Craftsmen's Council, 1965.

Spargo, John. *Early American Pottery and China.* New York: The Century Company, 1926.

———. *The Potters and Potteries of Bennington.* New York: Houghton Mifflin, 1926.

Sparkes, John C.L., and Gandy, Walter. *Potters: Their Arts and Crafts.* London: S.W. Partridge and Co., 1896.

Watkins, Lura Woodside. *Early New England Potters and their Wares.* Sturbridge, Massachusetts: Old Sturbridge Village, 1959.

Watkins, C. Malcolm, and Hume, Ivor Noel. *The Poor Potter of Yorktown.* Washington, D.C.: Smithsonian Institution Press, 1967.

Webster, Donald. *Decorated Stoneware Pottery of North America.* Rutland, Vermont and Tokyo, Japan: Charles E. Tuttle and Co., 1971.

———. *Early Canadian Pottery.* Greenwich, Connecticut: New York Graphic Society, Inc., 1971.

Wiltshire, William E. III. *Folk Pottery of the Shenandoah Valley.* New York: E.P. Dutton and Co., Inc., 1975.

Articles

"ABC's of Good Salt Glazing." *Brick and Clay Record*, September, 1943, pp. 25–29.

Boney, Knowles. "Study of a Group of English Salt-Glaze Ware." *Antiques*, December, 1965 pp. 834–837.

MacFarlane, Janet R. "Nathan Clark, Potter." *Antiques*, LX (July, 1951), pp. 42–44.

Remensnyder, John. "The Potters of Poughkeepsie." *Antiques*, July, 1966, 90–95.

Troy, Jack. "Fuming in the Salt Kiln." *Craft Horizons*, June, 1972, p.28.

Unpublished MFA Theses

Littell, Duane. "Salt Glazing and Related Techniques." Graduate School, College of Ceramics, Alfred University, Alfred, New York.

Zamek, Jeff. "Sodium Carbonate Vapor Firing." Graduate School, College of Ceramics, Alfred University, Alfred, New York.

Catalogs

Freeman, John Crosby. *Blue Decoarted Stoneware of New York State.* Old Ireland P.O. Watkins Glen, N.Y.: American Life Foundation, 1966.

Ketchum, William C. Jr. *The Pottery of the State.* New York: New York Museum of American Folk Art, 1974.

Loar, Peggy. *Indiana Stoneware.* Indianapolis: Indianapolis Museum of Art, 1974.

Salt Glaze Ceramics. New York: American Crafts Council, 1972 (currently available).

References

Handbook of Chemistry and Physics. Cleveland: Chemical Rubber Publishing Company.

North American Combustion Handbook. Cleveland: North American Manufacturing Company.

Parmelee, Cullen, *Ceramic Glazes.* Chicago: Industrial Publications, 1948.

Rhodes, Daniel, *Kilns, Design, Construction and Operation.* Philadelphia: Chilton Book Company, 1968.

MATERIALS SUPPLIERS

Alundum and Silicon-Carbide Shelves and Posts

Carborundum Co.
Refractories Division
P.O. Box 339
Niagara Falls, NY 14302
district offices throughout
the United States and Canada

Engineered Ceramics
Division of Sola Basic Ind.
P.O. Box 1
Gilberts, ILL 60136

Norton Co.
Refractories Division
Worchester, MA 01606

Atmospheric Burners

Gas Appliance Co.
20909 Brant Ave. So.
Long Beach, CA 90810

Johnson Gas Appliance Co.
Cedar Rapids, IO 52405

Westwood Ceramic Supply Co,
14400 Lomitas Ave.
City of Industry, CA 91744

Ceramic-fiber Products

Babcock and Wilcox
Old Savannah Rd.
Augusta, GA 30903

Carborundum Co.
P.O. Box 324
Tuxedo, NY 10987
district offices throughout
the United States and Canada

Johns-Manville
22 E. 40th St.
New York, NY 10016
district offices throughout
the United States and Canada

Refractory Products Co.
550 W. Central Rd.
Mt. Prospect, ILL 60056
(ceramic-fiber blanket available
in small quantities)

Superamics
P.O. Box 8363
Medeira Beach, FL 33738
(ceramic-fiber insulation
available in small quantities)

Thermo Engineering Co.
5105 Buffalo Ave.
P.O. Box 3935
Jacksonville, FL 32206

Mineral Wool Block

Babcock and Wilcox
Old Savannah Rd.
Augusta, GA 30903
district offices throughout
the United States and Canada

Moldatherm

Vacuum-formed Kilns and Furnaces
Lindberg
304 Hart St.
Watertown, WIS 53094

Refractory Products

A.P. Green Refractories Co.
1018 E. Breckenridge St.
Mexico, MI 65265
district offices throughout
the United States, Canada,
and the world

Babcock and Wilcox
Old Savannah Rd.
Augusta, GA 30903
district offices throughout
the United States, Canada,
and the world

Safety Solenoid Gas Cutoff Systems

General Controls ITT
801 Allen Ave.
Glendale, CA 91201

Safety Glasses

Best and least expensive are #2
welder's green lenses available
from any welding supply center

Sodium Silicate

Fisher Scientific Co.
633 Greenwich St.
New York, NY 10014
district offices throughout
the United States and Canada

Stannous Chloride

Least expensive grade available
from college or university chemistry
supply centers

Vari-Form-B and LDS Mixes —Boron Ceramic Fibers

Carborundum Co.
P.O. Box 339
Niagara Falls, NY 14302
district offices throughout the
United States, Canada, and the world

Monsanto Chemicals Ltd.
10-18 Victoria St.
London, SW1, England

Monsanto Australia Pty. Lt.
65 Bourke Rd.
Alexandria, N.S.W. 2015
Australia

British Ceramic Suppliers

E.J. Arnold & Sons Ltd.
Butterley St., Leeds 10

Craftsmen Potters Association
William Blake House, Marshall St.
London W.1

Ferro (Gt. Britain) Ltd.
Wombourne
Wolverhampton, Staffs

Fraser Ltd., Keramos
Parkside, Trentham
Stoke-on-Trent, Staffs

Fulham Pottery Ltd.
210 New Kings Rd.
Fulham, London S.W.6

Harrison/Mayer Ltd. Meir
Stoke-on-Trent, Staffs

Larbert Supplies & Maintenence Ltd.
18 Main St.
Stirlingshire, Scotland

Podmore & Sons Ltd.
Shelton
Stoke-on-Trent, Staffs

Potclays Ltd.
Wharf St.
Stoke-on-Trent, Staffs

Pottery Centre of Ireland Ltd.
95 St Stephen's Green
Dublin 2, Ireland

South Wales Art & Craft Supplies
108 Bute St.
Cardiff

INDEX

Numbers in italics refer to illustrations